Countries around the World

A Children's Picture Book about the Different Countries around the World

A Great Simple Picture Book for Kids to Learn about the Different Countries around the World

Melissa Ackerman

PUBLISHED BY:

Melissa Ackerman

Disclaimer

The information contained in this book is for general information purposes only. The information is provided by the authors and while we endeavor to keep the information up to date and correct, we make no representations or warranties of any kind, express or implied, about the completeness, accuracy, reliability, suitability or availability with respect to the book or the information, products, services, or related graphics contained in the book for any purpose. Any reliance you place on such information is therefore strictly at your own risk.

TABLE OF CONTENTS

Afghanistan

Official Name: Islamic Republic of Afghanistan

Capital City: Kabul

Afghanistan is a country from Central Asia. It is regarded as a landlocked country or a country entirely enclosed by land - Pakistan in the south and east; Iran in the west; Turkmenistan, Uzbekistan, and Tajikistan in the north. Based on the estimations of the United Nations (an organization that promotes international cooperation), Afghanistan has a total population of 33,369,945 as of July 1, 2016. Its territory has an area of 652,000 km2, making Afghanistan the 41st largest country in the world. Surprisingly, the New Year in Afghanistan, called Nowruz

, is celebrated on 21 March, the first day of spring. The Nowruz is also known as Farmer's Day, with celebration lasting for two weeks. The Guli Surkh festival or the Red Flower (Red Tulip) Festival is the principal festival for Nowruz.

Albania

Official Name: Republic of Albania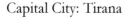

Capital City: Tirana

Albania is a country in Southeast Europe. It has a total area of 28,748 km2 and an estimated population of only 2,903,700 as of 2016. This particular country also ranks high when it comes to life expectancy, education, and income. It provides a universal health care system and free primary as well as secondary education. The only national airport in Albania is located in Tirana. This airport, the Tirana International Airport Nënë Tereza (image above) was named in 2001 after Mother Teresa to commemorate her work with the poor. Mother Teresa is an Albanian Roman Catholic nun and missionary well-known for her humanitarian work. She received the Nobel Peace Prize in 1979.

Algeria

Official Name: People's Democratic Republic of Algeria

Capital City: Algiers

Algeria is a state located in North Africa. It is considered as the tenth-largest country in the world, with its 2,381,741 km2 total area. And as of July 1, 2016, UN estimated that Algeria has a population of about 40,375,954. It is also known a semi-presidential republic where the government is headed by a president along with a prime minister. In addition, Algeria is made up of 48 provinces and 1,541 communes. Annaba (image above), one of the largest cities in Algeria is best-known for its beaches that lie on the coast of the Mediterranean Sea. This city serves as a major port and a popular tourist centre. Aside from its beaches, Annaba also has a lively night life.

Andorra

Official Name: Principality of Andorra

Capital City: Andorra la Vella

Andorra is a sovereign microstate or a small independent state that is recognized by larger states in Southwestern Europe. It is a landlocked microstate bordered by Spain and France. It is also called "principality" as it is headed by two Co-Princes – the Spanish/Roman Catholic Bishop of Urgell and the President of France. Andorra's total area is 467.63 km2, and as of July 1, 2016, it has a population of only 69,165. Its capital city, the Andorra la Vella (image above) is the highest capital city in Europe, with an elevation of 1,023 meters above sea level. Due to its high location, this small but beautiful city is very near to world class ski resorts. In 2013, the people of Andorra had the highest life expectancy in the world at 81 years, according to The Lancet, a scientific journal.

Angola

Official Name: Republic of Angola

Capital City: Luanda

Angola is a country located in Southern Africa. It is the 23rd largest country in the world, with its 1,246,700 km2 total area. As of July 1, 2016, this country has an estimated population of 25,830,958, according to United Nations. Angola has huge mineral and petroleum reserves. In fact, its economy is among the fastest growing in the world, with oil and diamonds being its primary sources of income. With its vast resources, Angola has become China's major oil supplier. The Morena Beach (image above), which is located in Benguela, Angola is a part of the Atlantic Ocean and is one of the best known beaches in Angola. It is located near the city and is also much visited for its beauty.

Antigua and Barbuda

Official Name: Antigua and Barbuda

Capital City: Antigua

Antigua and Barbuda is a twin-island country in the Americas. It is located between the Caribbean Sea and the Atlantic Ocean. Aside from the two major islands (Antigua and Barbuda), it also has several smaller islands such as, Great Bird, Green, Guinea, Long, Maiden and York Islands and Redonda. It has a total are of only 440 km2, with an estimated population of 92,738 as of July 1, 2016. In addition, Antigua and Barbuda has been given the nickname "Land of 365 Beaches" due to the many beaches (image above) surrounding its islands.

Argentina

Official Name: Argentine Republic

Capital City: Buenos Aires

Argentina is a nation located in southeastern portion of South America. It is considered as the 8th largest country in the world with its 2,780,400 km2 total mainland area. As of July 1, 2016, it has an estimated population of 43,847,277. Argentina is also made up of 23 provinces and one city – the Buenos Aires, which has become the country's capital city. Argentina is regarded as a high-income economy. The famous Tango (image above), a sensual ballroom dance performed by a man and a woman originates in and is a signature art of Buenos Aires.

Armenia

Official Name: Republic of Armenia

Capital City: Yerevan

Armenia is a sovereign state in the region of Eurasia, the combined landmass of Europe and Asia. It has a total area of 29,743 km2 and an estimated population of 3,026,048 (as of July 1, 2016). Unknown to many, Armenia is considered as the first state in the world to adopt Christianity as its official religion. It was between the late 3rd century and early years of the 4th century when the state became the first Christian nation. The Armenian Apostolic Church (image above), which was noted as the world's oldest national church is located in Armenia. This county also lies in the highlands surrounding the Biblical mountains of Ararat, upon which Noah's Ark came to rest after the Great Flood.

Australia

Official Name: Commonwealth of Australia

Capital City: Canberra

Australia is a developed country from the Australian continent. It is the world's sixth largest country with its 7,692,024 km2 total area. It has an estimated population of 24,309,330 as of 2016. It is also considered as one of the wealthiest countries in the world. Australia also ranks highly when it comes to quality of life, health, education, economic freedom, and the protection of civil liberties and political rights. Surprisingly, most of Australia's exotic flora (flower) and fauna (animal) cannot be found anywhere else in the world. The Koala (image above), for example, which is a tree-dwelling mammal, originates in Australia.

Austria

Official Name: Republic of Austria

Capital City: Vienna

Austria is a nation located in Central Europe which is highly mountainous. It is a landlocked country bordered by the Czech Republic and Germany to the north, Hungary and Slovakia to the east, Slovenia and Italy to the south and Switzerland and Liechtenstein to the west. It has about 83,879 km2 total area and an 8,569,633 estimated population in 2016. Just like Australia, Austria is also regarded as one of the richest countries in the world, with a high standard of living. Vienna's Central Cemetery (image above) has over 2.5 million tombs, which is more than the city's live population. Some of the famous people buried in the said cemetery include Beethoven, Brahms, Gluck, Schubert, Schoenberg and Strauss.

Azerbaijan

Official Name: Republic of Azerbaijan

Capital City: Baku

Azerbaijan is a country located at the crossroads of Southwest Asia and Southeastern Europe. This country does not have an official religion. However, people in Azerbaijan practice secularism or the separation of government institutions and religious institutions. Some also adhere to Shia Islam, a branch of Islam. It also has an estimated population (as of 2016) of 9,868,447 and a total land area of 86,600 km2. In addition, the Yanar Dag or burning mountain (image above) can also be found in Azerbaijan. This particular mountain continuously burn due to natural gas present on the soil.

Bahamas

Official Name: Commonwealth of the Bahamas

Capital City: Nassau

The Bahamas is an archipelagic state or a state that is made up of more than 700 islands, cays (small sandy islands) and islets (very small islands). It can be found at the Atlantic Ocean. It has a total area of 13,878 km2, 28% of which is water. It also has an estimated population of only 392,718 as of 2016. One of the best tourist attractions of Bahamas is the Dean's Blue Hole (image above), the world's deepest known salt water vertical blue hole. It is about 202 meters deep and is located in the west of Clarence Town on Long Island, Bahamas.

Bahrain

Official Name: Kingdom of Bahrain

Capital City: Manama

Bahrain is an island country located at the west of the Persian Gulf in the Middle East. This country is noted as the site of the ancient Dilmun civilization, one of the oldest civilizations in the Middle East. It also considered as one of the earliest areas to convert to Islam. It has a total area of only 765 km2 and a 2016 estimated population of 1,396,829. Furthermore, Bahrain is popular for its 400-year-old mesquite tree which is also known as 'The Tree of Life' (image above). This particular tree surrounded by nothing but desert is able to live for many years as its roots stretches at about 160 feet deep. Because of this, Bahrain is considered as one of the many supposed locations of the Garden of Eden.

Bangladesh

Official Name: People's Republic of Bangladesh

Capital City: Dhaka

Bangladesh is a country located in South Asia. It is considered as the world's eighth-most populous country, with its 162,910,864 estimated population in 2016. The total area of its territory is 147,570 km2 only. Three of Asia's largest rivers, the Ganges, the Brahmaputra and the Meghna, can also be found in this country. Bangladesh is also home to 700 more rivers and to one of the world's longest beaches – the Cox's Bazar (image above), with a 600 kilometers coastline.

Barbados

Official Name: Barbados

Capital City: Bridgetown

Barbados is an island country located in the Americas and surrounded by the Pacific Ocean. Sometimes, it is called Little England. It has a total area of only 439 km2 and an estimated population of 285,006 (as of July 2016). It is also noted as one of the leading tourist destinations. In addition, Barbados is actually a coral island or a type of island formed from fragments of dead corals and other organic materials. Because it is a coral island the beaches are nicer than many other islands.

Belarus

Official Name: Republic of Belarus

Capital City: Minsk

Belarus or Byelorussia is a landlocked country located in Eastern Europe. It is bordered by: Russia to the northeast, Ukraine to the south, Poland to the west, Lithuania and Latvia to the northwest. It has a total area of 207,595 km2, most of which is forested. As of 2016, its estimated population is around 9,481,521. The Belovezhskaya Pushcha National Park (image above) in Belarus is a preserved part of the Białowieża Forest – one of the last and largest remaining parts of the primeval forest, a virgin forest or a very old forest that has not been significantly disturbed.

Belgium

Official Name: Kingdom of Belgium

Capital City: Brussels

Belgium is a state that can be found in Western Europe. It is a small country which covers an area of 30,528 km2. Its population, as of 2016, is around 11,371,928. This particular country is also divided into three regions: Dutch-speaking region of Flanders, French-speaking southern region of Wallonia and the bilingual Brussels-Capital Region. Interestingly, Belgium is also home to Europe's oldest shopping arcades – the Galeries Royales Saint-Hubert (image above) in Brussels, which first opened in 1847.

Belize

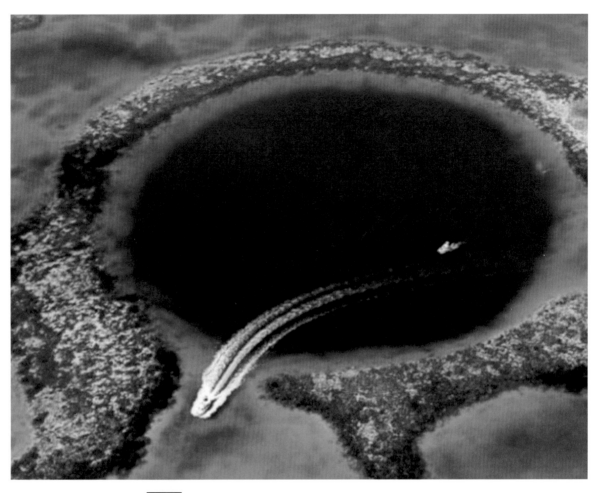

Official Name: Belize

Capital City: Belmopan

Belize is a country on the eastern coast of Central America. It is the only country in Central America whose official language is English and not the usual Spanish. However, Spanish is also commonly spoken in this country. With its 22,966 km2 land area and a population of 366,942 as of 2016, Belize is noted for having the lowest population density in Central America. Belize is known for its September Celebrations (Independence Day and National Day), its extensive coral reefs, and its music. However, the major tourist attraction in Belize is the Great Blue Hole (image above) – an underwater sinkhole, surrounded by corals. It is about 124 meters deep and was believed to be the world's largest underwater sinkhole. It is also home to several types of fish, like basking sharks.

Benin

Official Name: Republic of Benin

Capital City: Porto-Novo

Benin is a country in West Africa. Though the country's capital is Porto-Novo, the seat of government is located in Cotonou, the country's largest city. It covers an area of 114,763 km2, while its population in 2016 was estimated to be around 11,166,658. The official language in this country is French. However, native languages such as Fon and Yoruba are also commonly used. One of the major tourist attractions in Benin is the Royal Palaces of Abomey (image above). This site is actually made up of 12 palaces spread over a 40 hectares area at the heart of the Abomey town in Benin, which is formerly the capital of the ancient Kingdom of Dahomey. However, when the town was hit by a tornado on March 15, 1984, most of the palaces were damaged.

Bhutan

Official Name: Kingdom of Bhutan

Capital City: Thimphu

Bhutan is a state located in South Asia. Its official religion is Vajrayana Buddhism, while the national language is Dzongkha. Its total land area is about 38,394 km2. Its 2016 population on the other hand is approximately 784,103. As part of Bhutan's effort to preserve its culture, citizens of Bhutan are required to follow a specific dress code in public. Men typically wear a robe called a gho while the women wear dresses called kira (image above).

Bolivia

Official Name: Plurinational State of Bolivia

Capital City: Sucre

Bolivia is a landlocked country in South America. It is surrounded by different countries including: Brazil, Paraguay, Argentina, Chile and Peru. The total are of this country is 1,098,581 km2, one-third of which is covered by the Andean mountain range. As of 2016, Bolivia has an estimated population of 10,888,402 which is multiethnic and includes Amerindians, Mestizos, Europeans, Asians and Africans. The official language in the country is Spanish. However, 36 other native languages are also being used. Amusingly, one of the main tourist attractions in the country is the Eduardo Abaroa Andean Fauna National Reserve which is located in Sur Lípez Province in Bolivia. It is regarded as the country's most visited protected area. This is also where the Árbol de Piedra or "stone tree" (image above) can be found. The Árbol de Piedra is actually is an unusual rock formation, about 7 meters high, and was unbelievably formed by wind-blown sand.

Bosnia and Herzegovina

Official Name: Bosnia and Herzegovina

Capital City: Sarajevo

Bosnia and Herzegovina is a country in Southeastern Europe. It has a land area of 51,197 km2 and a population of 3,802,134. It ranks high when it comes to literacy, life expectancy and education levels. It is also considered as one of the most frequently visited countries with its natural beauty, culture, cuisine, music, architecture and festivals. Its capital city, the Sarajevo (image above) is breathtakingly beautiful that the travel guide series, Lonely Planet, named Sarajevo as the 43rd best city in the world. This city has also been listed as one of the top ten cities to visit in 2010.

Botswana

Official Name: Republic of Botswana

Capital City: Gaborone

Botswana is a country located in Southern Africa. The citizens on this country were called Batswana. Its land area is 581,730 km2, while the country's 2016 population is estimated to be at around 2,303,820. The Kalahari Desert (image above), a large semi-arid sandy savanna in southern Africa covers approximately 84% of Botswana. In comparison to other deserts, the Kalahari is a home to more animals and plants.

Brazil

Official Name: Federative Republic of Brazil

Capital City: Brasilia

Brazil is the largest country in South America and Latin America. It is considered as the world's fifth-largest country with a total area of 8,515,767 km2. It is also regarded as the fifth most populous country in the world, with approximately 209,567,920 population as of 2016. Brazil is, as well, one of the world's richest countries with a fast growing major economy until 2010. The original capital city of Brazil was Rio de Janeiro. However, in 1891 it was stated that the capital should be moved from Rio de Janeiro to a place close to the country's center. And so, a new city was designed and built to serve as Brazil's new capital city, which will be called, Brasilia (image above). The city was developed and built in one of the country's highlands, with the construction lasting for 41 months. The inauguration of this newly-built city happened in 1960.

Brunei

Official Name: Nation of Brunei

Capital City: Bandar Seri Begawan

Brunei is a state located in the island of Borneo in Southeast Asia. It is the only complete state on the island of Borneo, covering a total area of 5,765 km2. The remainder of the island, not covered by Brunei is divided between Malaysia and Indonesia. As of July 2016, Brunei's population was 428,874. The Istana Nurul Iman (image above), is the official residence of the Sultan of Brunei and the seat of the Brunei government. It is also considered as one of the "world's largest palace".

Bulgaria

Official Name: Republic of Bulgaria

Capital City: Sofia

Bulgaria is a country that can be found in southeastern Europe. Its territory covers a total area of 110,994 km2. As of 2016, its estimated population is approximately 7,097,796. Sofia, the capital of Bulgaria, was founded 7000 years ago. This makes it the second oldest city in Europe. Being the largest city in Bulgaria, it became a home to many of the major local universities, cultural institutions and commercial companies of the country.

Burkina Faso

Official Name: Burkina Faso

Capital City: Ouagadougou

Burkina Faso is a country in West Africa. It is surrounded by six countries: Mali, Niger, Benin, Togo, Ghana and Ivory Coast. It has a total area of 274,200 km2 and a population of 18,633,725 as of 2016. In addition, Burkina Faso is also regarded as a francophone or a French-speaking country. The Domes of Fabedougou is one of the country's tourist attractions. These domes are close to two billion years old rock formations made up of deposited layers of sandstone. It is possible to climb to the top of some of them.

Burundi

Official Name: Republic of Burundi

Capital City: Bujumbura

Burundi is a country located in East Africa. It is a landlocked country bordered by Rwanda, Tanzania and the Democratic Republic of the Congo. It has a total area of 27,834 km2 and an estimated population of about 11,552,561. The economy in the country is predominantly agricultural, with coffee and tea being Burundi's primary exports. One of the most visited places in Burundi is the Saga Beach (image above), which is part of the shore of Lake Tanganyika in Burundi. With its clear and white sand accompanied by sprawling waves, the Saga Beach is the most famous amongst the country's tourist destinations.

Cabo Verde

Official Name: Republic of Cabo Verde

Capital City: Praia

Cabo Verde or Cape Verde is an island country located in the central Atlantic Ocean. It has an estimated population of 526,993 and a total land area of 4,033 km2. This country has also been one of the most developed countries in Africa. And though it lacks natural resources, its economy is mostly service-oriented, focusing on tourism and foreign investment. One of the most interesting places in this country is the Chã das Caldeiras (image above) – a small community with about 1,000 inhabitants and is located within the crater of Pico do Fogo, the highest volcano in Cabo Verde.

Cambodia

Official Name: Kingdom of Cambodia

Capital City: Phnom Penh

Cambodia is a country in the Southeast Asia. It has about 181,035 km2 total area and a population of 15,827,241. The official religion in this country is Theravada Buddhism, a branch of Buddhism. The country also has one of the fastest growing economies in Asia, with agriculture being the dominant economic sector. Some other sources of income in this country includes: textiles, construction, garments, and tourism. Moreover, the Angkor Wat Temple (image above) is one of the major tourist attractions in Cambodia. It is also considered as one of the largest temple in the world and accounts for a significant number of international tourists every year.

Cameroon

Official Name: Republic of Cameroon

Capital City: Yaoundé

Cameroon is a country that can be found in West Africa. As of 2016, it has a population of 23,924,407, while its total area is around 475,442 km2. It is home to several beaches, deserts, mountains, rainforests, and savannas. The country is also famous for its native styles of music and for its successful national football team. One of the main tourist attractions in Cameroon is Limbe (image above) – a seaside city in the South-West Region of Cameroon. Aside from its beautiful black sand beaches, Limbe is also known for being the center of the country's oil industry.

Canada

Official Name: Canada

Capital City: Ottawa

Canada is a country located in North America. It is regarded as the world's second-largest country with a total area of 9,984,670 km2. Its estimated population on the other hand, is approximately 36,286,378 as of 2016. Most of its land territory is dominated by forest and the Rocky Mountains. Being a rich country, this particular country also ranks high when it comes to quality of life, economic freedom, and education. One of the "must-see" places in Canada is the CN Tower (image above) in Toronto. It is about 553 meters high and was considered as the tallest tower in the whole world.

Central African Republic

Official Name: Central African Republic

Capital City: Bangui

The Central African Republic is a country in Central Africa. It has a total area of 622,984 km2 and a population of 4,998,493. This country is rich in mineral deposits and other natural resources like diamonds, cobalt, uranium reserves, crude oil, gold, lumber, and hydropower. The Chutes De Boali (image above) - a series of spectacular waterfalls which is about 50 meters high is one of the most visited places in the Central African Republic.

Chad

Official Name: Republic of Chad

Capital City: N'Djamena

Chad is a country in Central Africa. It is bordered by six countries including: Libya, Sudan, Central African Republic, Cameroon, Nigeria and Niger. It has a total area of 1,284,000 km2 and a 14,496,739 estimated population. It is also noted as "the Dead Heart of Africa" due to its harsh dry desert climate. N'Djamena (image above), the capital and largest city of Chad is the home several attractions like Chad National Museum, cathedral and mosques and the spectacular sunset across Chari River.

Chile

Official Name: Republic of Chile

Capital City: Santiago

Chile is a country located in South America. It is a long, narrow strip of land that has a total area of 756,096.3 km2. As of July, 2016, its population was estimated to be around 18,131,850. This country is also rich is forests, volcanoes, lakes, canals, peninsulas (piece of land bordered by water on three sides but connected to land) and islands. One of the most popular attractions in Chile is the Easter Island (image above), a Chilean territory. This particular place is famed for its 887 giant stone figures, called moai, created many centuries ago.

China

Official Name: People's Republic of China

Capital City: Beijing

China is a country located in Asia. It is the considered as the world's most populous country, with a population of 1,382,323,332 as of July, 2016. This country is also regarded as the fourth-largest country with its 9,596,961 km2 total area. For the past two thousand years, China amazingly had one of the largest economies in the world. The Forbidden City (image above), a Chinese imperial palace which served as the home of emperors and their households for almost 500 years, is one of the country's main attraction. This palace was considered as one of the world's largest palace complex and a World Heritage Site. It is located in the center of Beijing, China and now houses the Palace Museum.

Colombia

Official Name: Republic of Colombia

Capital City: Bogota, D.C

Colombia is a country with territories located in both South America and Central America. It has a 1,141,748 km2 total area and a 48,654,392 estimated 2016 population. Muzo, a town and municipality in Boyacá Department, Colombia, is widely known for its emerald mines where the world's highest quality emeralds (image above) can be found. The Devonshire, one of the world's most famous uncut emeralds, is from the Muzo mines. This 1383.95 carat emerald was a gift to the 6th Duke of Devonshire by Emperor Dom Pedro I of Brazil in 1831.

Comoros

Official Name: Union of the Comoros

Capital City: Moroni

Comoros is an archipelago island nation or a chain of islands in the Indian Ocean. It is a small nation with a total area of only 2,034 km2. The population, on the other hand, is estimated at 807,118 as of 2016. This country also has three official languages including: Comorian, Arabic and French. Chomoni Beach (image above), a small beach in the east of Comoros is one of the best beaches in the country that has pretty white sand. The best time for relaxing on the beach of Chomoni is during the dry season from May to November.

Congo, Democratic Republic of the

Official Name: Democratic Republic of the Congo

Capital City: Kinshasa

The Democratic Republic of the Congo, which is also called DR Congo, DRC, Congo-Kinshasa or Congo is another country in Central Africa. From 1971 to 1997 the country is known as Zaire. It is also noted as the second largest country in Africa and the eleventh largest in the world with its 2,345,409 km2 total area. When it comes to population, this particular country has a population of 79,722,624, making it the eighteenth most populated country in the world as of 2016. Mount Nyiragongo (image above) – an active volcano in the Democratic Republic of the Congo, is one of the beautiful places in the country. Its main crater which is about two kilometers wide usually contains a lava lake.

Congo, Republic of the

Official Name: Republic of the Congo

Capital City: Brazzaville

The Republic of the Congo or the Congo Republic or Congo-Brazzaville, is a country in Central Africa. It has a population of 4,740,992 and a total area of about 342,000 km2. This country is also the fourth largest oil producer in the Gulf of Guinea, the northeastern most part of the tropical Atlantic Ocean. The Congo River (image above), which can be found in the country, is considered as the second largest river in the world and the world's deepest river with depths, of over 220 meters.

Costa Rica

Official Name: Republic of Costa Rica

Capital City: San Jose

Costa Rica is a country located in Central America with a total area of 51,100 km2. As of 2016, it has a population of 4,857,218, nearly a quarter of which, live in the country's capital city, San José. This country was ranked twice of the New Economics Foundation's (NEF) as the best performing country when it comes to environmental sustainability. It has also been identified by the NEF as the greenest country in the world in 2009. The Monteverde Cloud Forest Biological Reserve (image above), serves as one of the most "must-visit" destinations in Costa Rica. Shrouded in a unique misty cover, this biological reserve has a mystical feel to it.

Cote d'Ivoire

Official Name: Republic of Côte d'Ivoire

Capital City: Yamoussoukro

Côte d'Ivoire or Ivory Coast is a country in West Africa. It has two capital cities: Yamoussoukro is the political capital, while the Abidjan serves as the economic capital. The country also has 322,463 km2 total area and a population of about 23,254,184. One of the must-see attractions in Côte d'Ivoire is St. Paul's Cathedral in Abidjan (image above). This modern church is laid out in a stylized version of the figure of St. Paul with his robes flowing behind him.

Croatia

Official Name: Republic of Croatia

Capital City: Zagreb

Croatia is a state that covers a 56,594 km2 total area and a population of 4,225,001. Its Adriatic Sea coast is made up of more than a thousand islands. The International Monetary Fund (an international organization), cited that Croatia has an emerging, developing and a high-income economy. The Plitvice Lakes National Park (image above), is one of the oldest national parks in Southeast Europe and the largest national park in Croatia. It is world famous for its lakes arranged in cascades. Currently, there are 16 lakes in the park which can be seen when viewed from above.

Cuba

Official Name: Republic of Cuba

Capital City: Havana

Cuba is a state located in the northern Caribbean. It is considered as the largest island in the Caribbean, with an area of 109,884 km2. As of July 2016, its population was estimated to be around 11,392,889. When it comes to performance, this country ranks highly in health care and education. Habana Vieja or Old Havana (image above), which can be found in Havana, Cuba is a UNESCO world heritage site. It is a well-preserved slice of Cuban history that gives a hint on how life in the country was like 200 years ago.

Cyprus

Official Name: Cyprus

Capital City: Nicosia

Cyprus is an island country located in the Eastern Mediterranean Sea. It has 9,251 km2 total area and a population of 1,176,598, making it the third largest and third most populous island in the Mediterranean Sea, which is a sea connected to the Atlantic Ocean. Being a major tourist destination, this country has a high-income economy. Interestingly, Khirokitia (image above), a site on Cyprus which dated back from roughly 10,000 years age was known as one of the most important and best preserved prehistoric sites of the eastern Mediterranean. It has been listed as a World Heritage Site by UNESCO since 1998. It features old buildings and settlements that are basically round in shape and has flat roofs.

Czech Republic

Official Name: Czech Republic

Capital City: Prague

The Czech Republic is a state found in Central Europe. It covers an area of 78,866 km2 and has a population of 10,548,058. This country is highly developed with an advanced, high income economy and high living standards. The Czech Republic is also regarded as the 6th most peaceful country. The Hluboká Castle (image above), is a historic castle located in Hluboká nad Vltavou. Considered as one of the most beautiful castles in the Czech Republic, it is a must-visit place for all romantics and history lovers.

Denmark

Official Name: Kingdom of Denmark

Capital City: Copenhagen

Denmark is a country located in Europe. It has an area of 42,925.46 km2 and a population of 5,690,750. It is made up of a peninsula and a chain of 443 named islands. The country is also regarded as the least corrupt country in the world, with a high-income economy. The Little Mermaid (image above), which is a bronze displayed on a rock by the waterside in Copenhagen, Denmark was the country's most famous landmark. It is about 1.25 meters tall and weighs around 175 kilograms. The statue was based on the fairy tale of the same name by Danish author Hans Christian Andersen.

Djibouti

Official Name: Republic of Djibouti

Capital City: Djibouti City

23,200 km2

Djibouti is a country located in the Horn of Africa (a peninsula in Northeast Africa). It occupies a total area of 23,200 km2, with an estimated population of only 899,598. Its official languages are Arabic and French. And for more than 1,000 years, most of the residents in the country adhere to Islam. One of the famous destinations in Djibouti is the Lac Assal – the saltiest lake outside of Antarctica and second saltiest all over the world.

Dominica

Official Name: Commonwealth of Dominica

Capital City: Roseau

Dominica is an island country that covers an area of 750 km2. The population here is around 73,016 only. It has also been nicknamed as the "Nature Isle of the Caribbean" due to its natural beauty. Mountainous rainforests can be found in this country which houses many rare plants, animals, and birds. One of the tourist attractions in Dominica is the Boiling Lake (image above) – the world's second-largest hot spring. It can be found in the Morne Trois Pitons National Park, Dominica's World Heritage site. It is filled with bubbling grayish-blue water and is usually covered in a cloud of vapor.

Dominican Republic

Official Name: Dominican Republic

Capital City: Santo Domingo

The Dominican Republic is a state in the Caribbean region. It has a 48,442 km2 total area and a population of 10,648,613 (as of 2016). Over the years, this country has been considered as having one of the fastest growing economies in the Americas. The Dominican Republic is also noted as one of the most visited destination in the Caribbean. Larimar (image above), a semi-precious stone is one of the great things that can only be found in the Dominican Republic. This rare stone which is also known as the "Atlantis Stone" or the "Stefilia's Stone" varies in coloration from white, light-blue, green-blue to deep blue.

East Timor

Official Name: Democratic Republic of Timor-Leste

Capital City: Dili

East Timor or Timor-Leste is a state in Southeast Asia which is about 15,410 km2 in size. As of 2016, the population in the country was estimated to be around 1,211,245. Along with the Philippines, it is one of only two predominantly Christian nations in Southeast Asia. Jaco Island (image above), is an uninhabited island in East Timor. It is separated from the mainland of the country by a beach. It is covered mainly by tropical dry forest, fringed by strand vegetation and sandy beaches.

Ecuador

Official Name: Republic of Ecuador

Capital City: Quito

Ecuador is a nation in northwestern South America. It covers a total area of 283,560 km2 and a population of about 16,385,450. The official language in the country is Spanish. It has also been classified as a medium-income country, with its developing economy highly dependent on petroleum and agricultural products. One of the most interesting places to visit in Ecuador is the Darwin Arch (image above) located in the Darwin Island. It is considered as one of the best dive sites in the world where different sharks, sea turtles, manta rays, dolphins and large schools of fishes can be found.

Egypt

Official Name: Arab Republic of Egypt

Capital City: Cairo

Egypt is a country spanning from Africa to Asia. It has a total area of 1,010,407.87 km2 and a population of approximately 93,383,57, making it the fifteenth-most populous country in the world. Moreover, the Pyramid of Djoser (image above), or step pyramid is considered as the first pyramid built during the 27th century BC. It is made up of six mastabas (of decreasing size) or rectangular structures constructed out of mud-bricks or stone. Originally, this particular pyramid is 62 meters tall.

El Salvador

Official Name: Republic of El Salvador

Capital City: San Salvador

El Salvador is the smallest country in Central America, with a total area of only 21,041 km2. As of July, 2016, the population in this country was estimated to be around 6,146,419. There is only one UNESCO World Heritage Site in El Salvador: Joya de Ceren (image above). Joya de Cerén is a small farming village preserved remarkably intact and buried under layers of volcanic ash. When a volcano erupted in the year 200, the villagers evacuated the community. By the year 590, another volcano erupted and buried the village under 14 layers of ash. Fortunately, the villagers were able to escape in time, as no bodies have been found in the ruins.

Equatorial Guinea

Official Name: Republic of Equatorial Guinea

Capital City: Malabo

Equatorial Guinea is a country in Central Africa. It has a total area of 28,050 km2 and a population of 869,587. The country has also been considered as one of sub-Saharan Africa's largest oil producers. One of the most beautiful places in the country is the Arena Blanca (image above) – the only white beach on Bioko Island, Equatorial Guinea. During the dry season thousands of butterflies can be seen in this breathtaking beach.

Eritrea

Official Name: State of Eritrea

Capital City: Asmara

Eritrea is another country located in the Horn of Africa. It has a total area of 117,600 km2 and a population of approximately 5,351,680. The Great Mosque of Asmara (image above), is one of the major tourist attractions and religious places in Asmara, Eritrea. The mosque is considered as majestic and so, visitors are expected to cover their heads and it is mandatory for women to be covered from head to toe if entering the mosque premises.

Estonia

Official Name: Republic of Estonia

Capital City: Tallin

Estonia is a country in Northern Europe. It covers a total area of 45,339 km2 and has a population of only 1,309,104, making it one of the least-populous member states of the European Union (a union of 28 states located in Europe). Incredibly, the country also has an advanced, high-income economy and high living standards. One of the most famous tourist destinations in Estonia is the Piusa Caves (image above) – these are man-made cave systems where sands where mined for making glasses.

Ethiopia

Official Name: Federal Democratic Republic of Ethiopia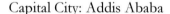

Capital City: Addis Ababa

Ethiopia is a state found in the Horn of Africa. With its 101,853,268 estimated population, the country became the most populous landlocked country in the world. It covers a total area of 1,104,300 km2, with Addis Ababa being its capital and largest city. In addition, this country has also been considered for having the 42nd most powerful military in the world, and the third most powerful in Africa. One of the interesting places in Ethiopia is the Danakil Depression (image above), which is located near the border with Eritrea and Ethiopia. It is considered as the hottest place on Earth in terms of year-round average temperatures. Additionally, the Danakil Depression contains sulfur springs or (yellowish) hot springs.

Fiji

Official Name: Republic of Fiji

Capital City: Suva

Fiji is an island country located in the South Pacific Ocean. It is an archipelago consisting of more than 330 islands and more than 500 islets. It has a total area of 18,274 km2 and a population of 897,537. The country also has one of the most developed economies in the Pacific, with tourist industry and sugar exports being its main sources. Interestingly, Taveuni, a small island in Fiji was cut straight through by the International Dateline, an imaginary line on the surface of the Earth that runs from the north pole to the south pole and set the boundaries of the change of one calendar day to the next. In the spot where the line runs, you will find a big Taveuni map that was split in two (image above) to mark both sides of the dateline. The gap is where tourists stand to be on both sides at once and get the obligatory tourist shot.

Finland

Official Name: Republic of Finland

Capital City: Helsinki

Finland is a state located in Europe. Its population was estimated to be around 5,523,904, as of July 2016. It is also noted as the eighth largest country in Europe, with a total area of 338,424 km2. In 2015, the country was ranked first as the most stable country in the world. Seeing the Northern Lights (image above) is a once-in-a-lifetime treat people look forward to when visiting Finland. Lapland, Finland's northernmost region is the best place to see these incredible blazing curtains of greenish light drape across the sky especially between September and March.

France

Official Name: French Republic

Capital City: Paris

France is a state located in Western Europe. It covers a total area of 643,801 km2 and has a total population of 64,668,129 as of 2016. In addition, the country has also been a center of art, science, and philosophy. In fact, the country was the third country in Europe with most cultural UNESCO World Heritage Sites. The famous Eiffel Tower (image above) in Paris was built as the entrance point for the 1889 World Fair, a large public exhibition held in Paris. It is one of the most visited monuments in Paris and all over the world.

Gabon

Official Name: Gabonese Republic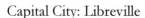

Capital City: Libreville

Gabon is a state located on the west coast of Central Africa. It has an area of 267,667 km2 and its population is estimated at 1,763,142 people as of 2016. The country is also regarded as one of the most prosperous countries in Sub-Saharan Africa with its low population, abundant petroleum, and foreign private investments. One of the main attractions in Gabon is the Ivindo National Park (image above) – the most remote of all the national parks in the country. This park is very well known for its unbelievable rapids and waterfalls and different kinds of animals such as birds, gorillas, chimps, mandrill, bush and pig.

Gambia

Official Name: Islamic Republic of the Gambia

Capital City: Banjul

Gambia is a country in West Africa. With a total area of 10,689 km2, it is regarded as the smallest country on mainland Africa. As of July, 2016, its population is around 2,054,986. The country's economy is dependent on farming, fishing, and tourism. One of the most interesting to visit and see in Gambia is the Wassu stone circles. These fascinating circles of standing stones around Wassu are noted as the most ancient man-made structures in the country, dating back to 1,200 years ago. The origin of these stone circles, which are 1-2.5 meters, is shrouded in mystery. However, it is believed that the stones are thought to mark the prehistoric burial grounds of a society long-since vanished.

Georgia

Official Name: Georgia

Capital City: Tbilisi

Georgia is a country located in Eurasia, a country in between Europe and Asia. It covers a territory of 69,700 km2 and its 2016 population was estimated to be around 3,979,781. One of the most famous spot in the country is the memorial statue of Savannah, Georgia's "Waving Girl" (image above). The popular "Waving Girl" is Florence Martus, who took it upon herself to be the unofficial greeter of all ships that entered and left the Port of Savannah, Georgia. At day, Martus would wave a handkerchief and a lantern by night. According to legend, Martus did not miss a single ship in her forty-four years on watch. It is believed that the reason she greeted ships was because she had fallen in love as a young girl with a sailor and wanted to be sure he would find her when he returned.

Germany

Official Name: Federal Republic of Germany

Capital City: Berlin

Germany is a state found in central-western Europe. It occupies an area of 357,168 km2 and has a population of approximately 80,682,351, making the country the sixteenth-most populous country in the world. Aside from having one of the world's richest economies, the country is also regarded as the world's third-largest exporter and importer of goods. The most photographed building in Germany, the Neuschwanstein Castle (image above), is one of the country's most popular tourist destinations. This breathtakingly beautiful fairy-tale castle served as the inspiration behind Walt Disney's Sleeping Beauty Castle. Constructed in the late 1800s, the Castle served as a fanciful retreat to King Ludwig II of Bavaria.

Ghana

Official Name: Republic of Ghana

Capital City: Accra

Ghana is a nation found in West Africa. It has a total area of 238,535 km2 and a population of 28,033,375. Amongst other countries in Africa, Ghana's economy is one of the strongest, most prosperous and most diversified. There are lots of tourist destinations in Ghana. However, the Busua Beach is one of the country's best beaches which offer the visitor a chance to relax and paddle in the Atlantic Ocean. There are several hotels along the beach front where visitors can stay. These hotels range from luxurious to simple.

Greece

Official Name: Hellenic Republic

Capital City: Athens

Greece or Hellas is a country in southeastern Europe. As of 2015, its population is approximately 10,919,459, while its territory is around 131,957 km2, eighty percent of which is mountainous. It addition, the country also has a high-income economy, a high quality of life and a very high standard of living. The very famous Mount Olympus (image above) is the highest mountain in Greece. It was notable in Greek mythology as the home of the Greek gods and goddesses. It is also noted for its unique plant types. Each year, thousands of people visit Mount Olympus to enjoy the scenery, tour its slopes and reach its peaks.

Grenada

Official Name: Grenada

Capital City: St. George's

Grenada is an island country located in the southeastern Caribbean Sea. Its territory covers an area of 348.5 km2. Its population in 2016 is approximately 107,327people. It was also well known as the "Island of Spice" because the country is one of the world's largest exporters of nutmeg. One of the main attractions in Grenada was the Seven Sisters Waterfalls or the St. Margaret's Falls (image above). The pools at these falls are nice and cold and are perfect place to beat the heat, or just relax with some friends on a picnic.

Guatemala

Official Name: Republic of Guatemala

Capital City: Guatemala City

Guatemala is a country in Central America that has a total area of 108,889 km2. It was bordered by Mexico, the Pacific Ocean, Belize, the Caribbean, Honduras and El Salvador. In 2016, it has an estimated population of 16,672,956. Its capital city is the Nueva Guatemala de la Asunción or Guatemala City. Antigua Guatemala (image above) is a city in Guatemala famous for its well-preserved Spanish Baroque-influenced architecture. Several ruins of colonial churches are also known to be found in this city. It has been designated a UNESCO World Heritage Site.

Guinea

Official Name: Republic of Guinea

Capital City: Conakry

Guinea is a country in West Africa which covers a total area of 245,836 km2. Its population in 2016 is around 12,947,122; 85 percent of which adheres to Islam. The country's economy is highly dependent on agriculture and mineral production. In fact, Guinea has been the world's second largest producer of bauxite, a soft substance that looks like clay from which aluminum is manufactured. In addition, the country also has rich deposits of diamonds and gold. The Conakry Grand Mosque (image above) located in Conakry, Guinea is Africa's fourth largest mosque that can accommodate 2,500 women on the upper level and 10,000 men on the lower level. It even has an extra room for 12,500 more worshippers at the grand esplanade. It is one of the top tourist attractions in Guinea because of its religious and cultural importance to the locals.

Guinea-Bissau

Official Name: Republic of Guinea-Bissau

Capital City: Bissau

Guinea-Bissau is a country in West Africa. Its territory occupies 36,125 km2 with an estimated population of 1,888,429. The main religions in the country are African traditional religions and Islam. However, there are a few people that adhere to Roman Catholic. One of the tourist attractions in Guinea-Bissau is the Fortress of Cacheu (image above). It was where Francis Drake, an English sea captain and John Hawkins, an English naval commander fought against the Portuguese in 1567. This fortress on the river which was built in 16th Century was restored in 2004 and contains some well-preserved guns.

Guyana

Official Name: Co-operative Republic of Guyana

Capital City: Georgetown

Guyana is a state in mainland South America. It covers a total area of 214,970 km2, making it the fourth-smallest country on mainland South America. The estimated population in this country is about 770,610 (as of 2016). Guyana is also the only nation in South America in which English is the official language. However, majority of the population speak Guyanese Creole. One of the best places in Guyana is the Orinduik Falls (image above). This waterfall cascades over solid, semi-precious jasper rocks to the beautiful relaxing river beneath. The rolling green hills surrounding this area add to the tranquility of one of Guyana's most beautiful waterfalls.

Haiti

Official Name: Republic of Haiti

Capital City: Port-au-Prince

Haiti is a state in North America which occupies a total area of 27,750 km2. Its estimated population is around 10,848,175 people, making it the second-most populous country in the Caribbean. The Citadelle Laferriere (image above) is a magnificent mountaintop fortress and one of the most beautiful places in Haiti that provides amazing views of the surrounding green fields. It was originally built after Haiti gained independence, in order to provide protection against French invasion. For Haitians, the fortress is a revered symbol of their strength when faced with threat.

Honduras

Official Name: Republic of Honduras

Capital City: Tegucigalpa

Honduras is a nation in Central America. Before, it was referred to as Spanish Honduras to differentiate it from British Honduras (now Belize). It covers an area of about 112,492 km2 and has a population of 8,189,501. In addition, the country is also known to be rich in various minerals, coffee, tropical fruit, and sugar cane, as well as for its textiles industry. The Copán Ruins Archeological Site (image above) which is found in Honduras is the most studied Maya city in the world. Maya people are Indian people from southeast Mexico, Guatemala, and Belize, whose civilization reached its height around the years 300-900. The Copán Ruins dated back to nearly 2,000 years ago. It is famous for the stelae (stone slab or column often used as a gravestone.) and altars that are scattered around the immense plaza.

Hungary

Official Name: Hungary

Capital City: Budapest

Hungary is a country in Central Europe. It has a total area of 93,030 km2 and a population around 9,821,318. The official language in the country is Hungarian.Being popular as a tourist destination, the country has a high-income economy. The Széchenyi Medicinal Bath (image above) in Budapest is one of the most visited places in Hungary. It is considered as the largest medicinal bath in Europe. Its water is supplied by two thermal springs with temperature about 74 °C and 77 °C. This thermal water has healing effects on joint illnesses, joint inflammations and orthopaedic and traumatological post-treatments. Generally, the water contains sulphate, calcium, magnesium, bicarbonate and a significant amount of fluoride acid and metaboric acid.

Iceland

Official Name: Republic of Iceland

Capital City: Reykjavík

Iceland is an island country located between the North Atlantic and the Arctic Ocean. It has a population of 331,778 and a total area of 102,775 km2. Its capital and largest city is Reykjavík, which, along with its surrounding areas in the southwest of the country houses more than two-thirds of the population. One of the most famous tourist destinations in Iceland is the Geysir or the Great Geysir (image above). It was the first known geyser to modern Europeans. The English word geyser which means, a periodically spouting hot spring was derived from Geysir. This ancient spring has been spewing boiling water up for at least 10,000 years that can reach heights of 70 meters in the air.

India

Official Name: Republic of India

Capital City: New Delhi

India is a country in South Asia which is about 3,287,263 km2 in size. With its population of around 1,326,801,576 people, it was regarded as the second-most populous country in the world. Currently, the Indian economy is the world's seventh-largest. The Taj Mahal (image above) is one of the most visited tourist destination in India. This structure is an ivory-white marble mausoleum commissioned by the Mughal emperor, Shah Jahan to house the tomb of his favorite wife, Mumtaz Mahal. It is considered as "the jewel of Muslim art in India and one of the universally admired masterpieces of the world's heritage"

Indonesia

Official Name: Republic of Indonesia

Capital City: Jakarta

Indonesia is a country in Southeast Asia, right between the Indian and Pacific Ocean. It covers an area of 1,904,569 km2, making it the largest island country. It is made up of more than thirteen thousand islands with an estimated population of over 258 million – the world's fourth most populous country. Tana Toraja, the home to the Toraja ethnic group is one of the most popular destinations in India. This place is located in between mountains and is simply unique. It has a very rich culture evident in its traditional villages and fascinating ceremonies that would wow visitors.

Iran

Official Name: Islamic Republic of Iran

Capital City: Tehran

Iran is a state in Western Asia which occupies a total area of 1,648,195 km2, making it the second-largest country in the Middle East. Its estimated population is approximately 80,043,146 people. Strategically located at the center of Eurasia and Western Asia, Iran is the only country with both a Caspian Sea and an Indian Ocean coastline. Persepolis (image above) is one of the most beautiful places in Iran. It served as the capital of the Achaemenid Empire or the First Persian Empire – the largest empire of ancient history. These ruins are also regarded as one of the world's most magnificent ancient sites.

Iraq

Official Name: Republic of Iraq

Capital City: Baghdad

Iraq is a 437,072 km2 country found in Western Asia. Its population is around 37,547,686, 95% of which are Shia or Sunni Muslims. However, other religious practices like Christianity, Yarsan, Yezidism, and Mandeanism are also present. The Ziggurat of Ur (image above) is one of the must-see places in Iraq. This ziggurat or rectangular stepped tower is one of the most well-preserved ziggurats built by King Ur-Nammu. At the top is a temple dedicated to honor Nanna, the patron deity of the city of Ur.

Ireland

Official Name: Republic of Ireland

Capital City: Dublin

Ireland is a state in north-western Europe which covers an area of 70,273 km2. Its estimated population is 4,713,993, around third of which live in Dublin. It is one of the top twenty-five wealthiest countries and the tenth most prosperous one in the world. Northern Ireland's only UNESCO World Heritage-listed site is the Giant's Causeway (image above). This very dramatic tourist attraction is a natural wonder made up of around 40,000 polygonal rock columns stretching along the coastline like a series of gigantic stepping stones. It is one of the country's most popular destinations, as visitors want to walk on its most peculiar pathways.

Israel

Official Name: State of Israel

Capital City: Jerusalem

Israel is a country located in the Middle East. It has about 22,072 km2 total area and a population of 8,192,463; 74.9 percent of which are Jewish. This country is also a developed country, with the 35th-largest economy in the world. It has the highest standard of living in the Middle East, the fourth highest in Asia and has one of the highest life expectancies in the world. The world renowned Dead Sea (image above) which is also called "The Sea of Death" or the Salt Sea is a lake in Israel. Considered as one of the world's saltiest bodies of water, anyone can easily float in the Dead Sea.

Italy

Official Name: Italian Republic

Capital City: Rome

59,801,004

Italy is a country in Europe that covers an area of 301,338 km2. As of July, 2016, its population was estimated to be around 59,801,004. It is the home to several famous scholars, artists, and polymaths like Leonardo da Vinci, Galileo, Michelangelo, and Machiavelli. Today, the country is regarded as having the eighth largest economy in the world, with a very high level of human development and high life expectancy. Pompeii (image above) is one of Italy's most visited tourist destinations. This famous Roman city was buried under several feet of volcanic ash for nearly 1,700 years. Its excavation began in 1748. However, the site is yet to be totally unearthed. Visitors can walk along the ancient streets of the city to see its remains.

Jamaica

Official Name: Jamaica

Capital City: Kingston

Jamaica is an island country in the Caribbean Sea. It has an area of 10,991 km2, making it the fourth-largest island country in the Caribbean. With a population around 2,803,362 people, this country is regarded as the fourth-most populous country in the Caribbean. Dunn's River Falls (image above) is one of Jamaica's most famous natural attractions. The falls tumble over rocks and limestone into the sea. Visitors can climb these tiered falls to the top with the aid of a guide. Visitors also enjoy the refreshing pools at the base of the falls.

Japan

Official Name: State of Japan

Capital City: Tokyo

Japan is another island country in East Asia. It is often called the "Land of the Rising Sun." Due to its location in the east, the country was believed to be the first land awakened by the rising sun. It covers an area of 377,972 km2, with an estimated population around 126,323,715. The country is also noted for having the world's third-largest economy. One of the 'must-see' in Japan is the blooming of Cherry Blossoms or Sakura. Hirosaki Castle Park (image above) is one of the best spots for viewing cherry trees. In fact, every year, there is a Hirosaki Cherry Blossom Festival celebrated from mid April to early May.

Jordan

Official Name: The Hashemite Kingdom of Jordan

Capital City: Amman

Jordan is an Arab kingdom in Western Asia. It covers an area of 89,341 km2, with a population around 7,747,800. It is also noted for being one of the safest Arab countries in the Middle East, keeping itself away from terrorism and instability, hence, making the country a major tourist destination. Wadi Rum (image above) which is also known as The Valley of the Moon is the largest wadi or valley in Jordan. Due to its reddish sands and rock formations, almost any movie about Mars had at least some of its scenes filmed in this region of Jordan.

Kazakhstan

Official Name: Republic of Kazakhstan

Capital City: Astana

Kazakhstan is a country in Central Asia. It occupies a territory of 2,724,900 km2, making it the world's largest landlocked country and the ninth largest in the world. As of 2016, the population in Kazakhstan was estimated to about 17,855,384. The country's economy is dependent on oil/gas industry, as well as in its rich mineral resources. Medeo (image above), is one of the best known tourist-destinations in Kazakhstan. It is an outdoor speed skating and bandy (team winter sport) rink. It is located in a mountain valley, making it the highest skating rink in the world.

Kenya

Official Name: Republic of Kenya

Capital City: Nairobi

Kenya is a country in Africa which occupies a total area of 581,309 km2. As of 2016, its population is around 47,251,449. Among the countries in East and Central Africa, Kenya has the largest economy, with agriculture being a major factor. Aside from exporting tea and coffee, the country also exports fresh flowers to Europe. One of the most visited places in Kenya is the Hell's Gate National Park (image above). It is a tiny park with dramatic scenery, steep cliffs, rock columns and wildlife like lions, leopards, and cheetahs.

Kiribati

Official Name: Republic of Kiribati

Capital City: Tarawa

Kiribati is an island nation located in the central Pacific Ocean. It has a total area of 811 km2 and a population of only 114,405. This particular nation is made up of 33 atolls or ring-shaped islands, reef islands and one raised coral island named Banaba. One of the must-visit places in Kiribati is the Our Lady of the Rosary Church (image above), a Catholic church made of limestone and has an impressive size.

Kuwait

Official Name: State of Kuwait

Capital City: Kuwait City

Kuwait is a country in Western Asia covering an area of 17,820 km2 and with 4,007,146 inhabitants as of 2016. Its high income economy was due to its massive oil reserves which is regarded as the sixth largest in the world. In addition, the Kuwaiti dinar is the highest valued currency in the world. The Kuwait Towers (image above), are regarded as a landmark and symbol of modern Kuwait. They have distinctive blue-green 'globes' that hold millions of liters of water. The smallest tower, on the other hand is used to light up the other two.

Kyrgyzstan

Official Name: Kyrgyz Republic

Capital City: Bishkek

Kyrgyzstan is a landlocked country found in Central Asia. It has a 6,033,769 population and a total area of 199,951 km2. The official language in the country is Kyrgyz, which is closely related to the other Turkic languages. However, Russian language is also widely spoken in the country. One of the popular historical locations in Kyrgyzstan is Tash Rabat (image above) – an ancient caravanserai or a roadside inn where travelers could rest. It has 31 chambers that have a distinctive dome which look magnificent on pictures.

Laos

Official Name: Lao People's Democratic Republic

Capital City: Vientiane

Laos is a landlocked country in Mainland Southeast Asia. It was bordered by Myanmar, China, Vietnam, Cambodia and Thailand. It has a total area of 236,800 km2 and a population of 6,918,367. Pha That Luang (image above), is a gold-covered large Buddhist stupa or structure that contains relics or the remains of Buddhist monks or nuns. It is also being used as a place of meditation. It is regarded as a national symbol and the most important national monument in Laos.

Latvia

Official Name: Republic of Latvia

Capital City: Riga

Latvia is a country in Northern Europe and is one of the three Baltic States or states on the coast of the Baltic Sea. The other Baltic States are Estonia and Lithuania. It has 1,955,742 inhabitants, a territory of 64,589 km2 and an official language called Latvian. The country is also considered as a high income country. Vecrīga or Old Riga (image above) is the historical center and the heart of Riga – Latvia's capital city. It is famous for its old rich culture as well as churches and cathedrals.

Lebanon

Official Name: Lebanese Republic

Capital City: Beirut

Lebanon is a state in Western Asia bordered by Syria and Israel. It has a total area of 10,452 km2 and a population around 5,988,153 people. During the 1960s, the country's capital, Beirut, attracted so many tourists that it was known as "the Paris of the Middle East". The Baatara gorge waterfall (image above) is a waterfall in the Lebanon where the water drops 255 meters into the Baatara Pothole (a cave) right behind the three bridges.

Lesotho

Official Name: Kingdom of Lesotho

Capital City: Maseru

Lesotho is a landlocked country completely surrounded by South Africa. It is about 30,355 km2 in size and has a population of 2,160,309. Its capital and largest city is Maseru. The Kome Caves (image above) are cave dwellings or huts made out of mud. These caves are located in Berea, Lesotho and are still inhabited by the descendants of the original people who built the caves.

Liberia

Official Name: Republic of Liberia

Capital City: Moneovia

Liberia is a country on the West African coast. It covers an area of 111,369 km2 and has population of 4,615,222 people as of 2016, more than 95% of which belong to numerous tribes. One of the key attractions in Liberia is the Blue Lake which also called Bomi Lake. This particular lake is about 300 feet deep and is surrounded by mountains. The sun's reflection, give the lake its popular blue color.

Libya

Official Name: State of Libya

Capital City: Tripoli

Libya is a country located in North Africa. With an area of 1,759,541 km2, the country is considered as the fourth largest country in Africa. As of July, 2016, the population in the country is about 6,330,159 people. When it comes to economy, Libya has the 10th-largest oil reserves in the world. Leptis Magna (image above) was a prominent city of the Roman Empire established in tenth century BC. The site is one of the most spectacular and unspoiled Roman ruins and so, hundreds of tourists every year come to visit this place. It is also included in the top ten tourist places in Libya.

Liechtenstein

Official Name: Principality of Liechtenstein

Capital City: Vaduz

Liechtenstein is a microstate or a country or state that has a very small population and/or very small land area located in Central Europe. It is a constitutional monarchy, and is headed by the Prince of Liechtenstein. It has an area of just 160 km2 and an estimated population of only 37,776. The wooden Old Rhine Bridge (image above), is a one-of-a-kind structure. This 135 meters of unpainted bridge connects Vaduz, Liechtenstein and Sevelen, Switzerland. It only permits pedestrians and cyclists, to cross over its squeaky floorboards. Today, the bridge is rustic in appearance, adding to this unique border-crossing experience.

Lithuania

Official Name: Republic of Lithuania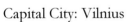

Capital City: Vilnius

Lithuania is a country in Northern Europe and is one of the three Baltic states. It has an estimated population of 2,850,030 million people as of 2016 and a total area of about 65,300 km2. The country has also been among the fastest growing economies in the European Union. One of the major attractions in Lithuania is the world renowned Hill of Crosses. It is a breathtaking sight that hosts more than two million crosses brought here by the people. Today, statues of the Virgin Mary, carvings of Lithuanian patriots and thousands of tiny rosaries are also being brought here by Catholics.

Luxembourg

Official Name: Grand Duchy of Luxembourg

Capital City: Luxembourg City

Luxembourg is a landlocked country in Western Europe bordered by Belgium, Germany and France. With an area of 2,586 km2, it is regarded as one of the smallest states in Europe. As of 2016, it has a population of 576,243, ranking it the 8th least-populous country in Europe. The Vianden Castle (image above), is one of the largest fortified castles in Luxembourg. It was built from the 11th to 14th centuries. Today, the castle is open to visitors from 10 am to 4 pm every day. In March and October, the closing time is extended to 5 pm, while during summer, it is open to public until 6 pm.

Macedonia

Official Name: Republic of Macedonia

Capital City: Skopje

Macedonia is a landlocked country in Southeast Europe bordered by Kosovo, Serbia, Bulgaria, Greece and Albania. It is about 25,713 km2 in size, with a population around 2,081,012 people. In addition, the country has more than fifty lakes and sixteen mountains higher than 2,000 meters. The Monastery of St. Naum (image above) located on a rocky cliff in Macedonia is a popular tourist attraction in the country. This Orthodox monastery was named after Saint Naum, a saint in the Orthodox Church.

Madagascar

Official Name: Republic of Madagascar

Capital City: Antananarivo

Madagascar is an island country located in the Indian Ocean. The 587,041 km2 territory of the country is consists of numerous smaller islands and the island of Madagascar, which is noted as the fourth-largest island in the world. As of 2016, its population is estimated to be around 24,915,822. Interestingly, more than 90% of the country's wildlife isn't found anywhere else on Earth. The Avenue of the Baobabs (image above), is a group of baobab trees lining the dirt road and is one of the most visited locations in Madagascar. There around 20 - 25 trees remaining that are approximately 30 meters in height. Its striking landscape attracts travelers from around the world.

Malawi

Official Name: Republic of Malawi

Capital City: Lilongwe

Malawi is a landlocked country located in southeast Africa. It is bordered by Zambia, Tanzania and Mozambique. It has a total area of 118,484 km2 with an estimated population of 17,749,826. Its economy is heavily dependent in agriculture. Lake Malawi (image above), is considered as the brightest jewel in Malawi's crown. It is about 29,600 km2 in size, with a depth of almost 300 meters. It is considered as the third largest lake in Africa. It is also one of the deepest lakes all over the world.

Malaysia

Official Name: Malaysia

Capital City: Kuala Lumpur

Malaysia is a monarchy located in Southeast Asia, wherein, the head of state is the king, known as the Yang di-Pertuan Agong, while the head of government is the prime minister. It has a total area of 330,803 km2 and a population of 30,751,602 people. The Petronas Twin Towers (image above), in Kuala Lumpur, Malaysia is a stand out structure deserved to be seen by tourists. These towers were the tallest buildings in the world until 2004. Today, these are still being considered as the world's tallest twin buildings, with a height of little over 450 meters. It features 88 floors of offices and a double-decker bridge which connects them on the 41st and 42nd floors.

Maldives

Official Name: Republic of Maldives

Capital City: Malé

Maldives is another island country in the Indian Ocean which is just 298 km2 in size. Its inhabitants are estimated to be around 369,812 people. Its capital city, Malé is traditionally called the "King's Island". According to the World Bank the country has an upper middle income economy dominated by tourism and fishing. The Artificial Beach (image above) in Maldives is a manmade beach in Malé which doesn't have a beach. This is created to provide a place for people to cool off and swim during the summer. It is a popular destination both to tourists and local residents. This white sandy artificial beach offers water sports and carnivals to its visitors.

Mali

Official Name: Republic of Mali

Capital City: Bamako

Mali is a landlocked country in West Africa. With a total area of 1,240,192 km2, the country is noted as the eighth-largest country in Africa. Its population, on the other hand, is around 18,134,835. The Great Mosque of Djenne (image above), which is found in Djenne, Mali is a famous destination. This mosque first built in the 13th century is the world's largest building to be constructed with mud brick. Today, the Great Mosque of Djenne is a sacred destination to many Muslims.

Malta

Official Name: Republic of Malta

Capital City: Valletta

Malta is an island country in Southern Europe. It covers an area of only 316 km2 with a population of just 419,615, making it one of the world's smallest country and one of the most densely populated countries. Due to its warm climate, this particular country is a popular tourist destination with several recreational areas, and architectural and historical monuments. Mdina (image above) is a fortified city in Malta. It was formerly the island's capital. Still confined within its walls, Mdina is now one of the main tourist attractions in Malta. The population in Mdina was estimated to be just under 300.

Marshall Islands

Official Name: Republic of the Marshall Islands

Capital City: Majuro

The Marshall Islands is an island country in the Pacific Ocean. Its population is approximately 53,069 spread out over the 181.43 km2 country. The country's wealth is dependent on a service economy, in fishing and in agriculture. The Bikini Atoll (image above) in Marshall Islands is an unusual and eerie place, as after the World War II, it was used as a ship graveyard. Also, this atoll has been used as a test location for many tests of nuclear bombs. Today, due to the bomb tests, the sunken ships in the lagoon are radioactive or emitting a powerful and dangerous form of energy called radiation.

Mauritania

Official Name: Islamic Republic of Mauritania

Capital City: Nouakchott

Mauritania is a country in North Africa where about 4,166,463 people inhabits. It is the eleventh largest country with its 1,030,000 km2 total area, about 90% of which is within the Sahara Desert. Chinguetti is an old town in Mauritania that does not have any shopping malls or theme parks, no tall buildings or any modern infrastructure. Its traditional and old-fashioned appeal attracts tourists from all over the world. Being in this town feels like being transported back in time.

Mauritius

Official Name: Republic of Mauritius

Capital City: Port Louis

Mauritius is an island nation located in the Indian Ocean. Its total area is 2,040 km2, while the population as of 2016 is approximately 1,277,459 people. It is known for its various plant and animal life. The Seven Coloured Earth (image above) is a major tourist attraction in Mauritius. It is made up of sand dunes of seven distinct colors including red, brown, violet, green, blue, purple and yellow. As the differently colored sands spontaneously settle in different layers, the sand dunes acquire a striped coloring. Interestingly, these sand dunes seemingly never erode despite the rains.

Mexico

Official Name: United Mexican States

Capital City: Mexico City

Mexico is a nation in North America bordered by the United States, Pacific Ocean, Guatemala, Belize, Caribbean Sea and Gulf of Mexico. It occupies a total area of 1,972,550 km2, making it the sixth largest country in the Americas. With an estimated population of 128,632,004, the country is regarded as the eleventh most populous country in the world. The ruins of the ancient city of Tulum (image above) is one of the country's most visited attractions. It is famous for its tall walls and was also considered as one of the last cities built and inhabited by the Maya.

Micronesia

Official Name: Federated States of Micronesia

Capital City: Palikir

Micronesia or Federated States of Micronesia is an island nation across the Western Pacific Ocean. It has around 607 islands which has a total land area of 702 km2. As of 2016, its estimated population is around 105, 014 people. The economy of this country mainly depends on farming and fishing. Chuuk (image above), is a state in Micronesia where most people come for scuba diving. It features astounding ships submerged from WWII, as well as beautiful and colorful corals.

Moldova

Official Name: Republic of Moldova

Capital City: Chiş inău

Moldova is a landlocked country in Eastern Europe. It is bordered by Romania and Ukraine. Its total area is around 33,846 km2, while its population in 2016 was estimated to be approximately 4,062,862 people. Soroca Fortress (image above) is a historic fort in Moldova, located in the city of Soroca – a breathtaking destination. This famed Soroca fortress is also a good example of ancient medieval architecture.

Monaco

Official Name: Principality of Monaco

Capital City: Monaco

Monaco is a city-state, or a state that has its own government and consists of a city and surrounding territory. It is bordered by France and by the Mediterranean Sea. It has an area of just 2.02 km2 and a population of about 37,863, making it the second smallest country in the world. Monaco-Ville (image above), which also called Le Rocher or The Rock, is the country's oldest town. It was built on a rocky land and may date back to the 6th century BC. It is made up of pedestrian streets and passageways, several hotels, restaurant, souvenir shops, the Prince's Palace, the Oceanographic Museum and St. Martin's Gardens.

Mongolia

Official Name: Mongolia

Capital City: Ulaanbaatar

Mongolia is a landlocked state in East Asia bordered by China and Russia. It has a total area of 1,566,000 km2, making it the world's second-largest landlocked country. As of July, 2016, the population in the country is around 3,006,444; 45% of which are in the capital city Ulaanbaatar. Lake Khövsgöl (image above), is known for being one of the clearest lakes in the whole world. It is about 36 km wide, 136 km long and 262 m deep. It is also bordered by mountains covered in forests.

Montenegro

Official Name: Montenegro

Capital City: Podgorica

Montenegro is a state in Southeastern Europe. It is about 13,812 km2 in size and the population is around 626,101 people only. When it comes to economy, this particular country is considered an upper middle-income country. The Lovcen National Park (image above), is a must see destination in Montenegro. At the top, it offers a magnificent view of the country. With its rocky appearance, this mountain is truly a unique piece of art.

Morocco

Official Name: Kingdom of Morocco

Capital City: Rabat

Morocco is a country located in North Africa. It is mountainous with large portions of desert. It has a population of 34,817,065 people and an area of 710,850 km2. The predominant religion in the country is Islam, while the official languages are Arabic and Berber. The Hassan II Mosque (image above), is a lavish symbol of Morocco itself. It features intricately carved marble pieces, vibrant mosaics and tile details completed by 10,000 artisans or skilled workers that make things using their hands.

Mozambique

Official Name: Republic of Mozambique

Capital City: Maputo

Mozambique is a country in Southeast Africa which has an area of 801,590 km2. It is bordered by the Indian Ocean, Tanzania, Malawi, Zambia, Zimbabwe, Swaziland and South Africa. As of 2016, the population in the country is around 28,751,362. The Bazaruto Island (image above), is a popular tourist destination in Mozambique. It has white sand beaches and dive spots. Manta ray, dolphins, turtles, and sharks can also be seen in the waters.

Myanmar

Official Name: Republic of the Union of Myanmar

Capital City: Naypyidaw

Myanmar, which is also known as Burma is a state in Southeast Asia. It is bordered by Bangladesh, India, China, Laos and Thailand. It covers an area 676,578 km2, while the population in 2016 was estimated around 54,363,426. The country is rich in jade, gems, oil, natural gas and other mineral resources. The Golden Rock or Kyaiktiyo Zedi (image above) is a totally incredible sight in Myanmar. It features a pagoda (a temple or sacred building) sitting atop a huge boulder that appears as if it's about to fall off the edge of a cliff. Both the pagoda and the rock are covered in golf leaf. The locals believe that the boulder is held in place through a miracle of Buddha, as the pagoda is said to contain a strand of his hair.

Namibia

Official Name: Republic of Namibia

Capital City: Windhoek

Namibia is a country in southern Africa bordered by the Atlantic Ocean, Zambia, Angola, Botswana and South Africa. Its territory covers an area of 825,615 km2, while the population is about 2,513,981 as of 2016. The country also enjoys high political, economic and social stability. Kolmanskop (image above), is a ghost town located in a desert in Namibia. In 1908, many Germans settled in this area after a diamond was found here. The German town that was built has different amenities and institutions including a hospital, ballroom, school, casino and a tram. However, in 1954, the town was completely abandoned when the diamond-field has been exhausted. Today, tourists can walk through the town and houses in knee-deep sand.

Nauru

Official Name: Republic of Nauru

Capital City: Yaren

Nauru which was formerly known as Pleasant Island is an island country in the Central Pacific. It only has 10,263 inhabitants in its 21 km2 territory. Overall, the country is a phosphate rock island, or an island with rich phosphate deposits near the surface. However, the phosphate reserves have been exhausted and the island's environment had been seriously harmed by mining. Today, one of the must-see destinations in Nauru is the Anibare District – the country's most beautiful tropical beach. It boasts a white coral sand coast and strong underwater currents and waves. Under the light of the full moon, the bay and beach are especially beautiful.

Nepal

Official Name: Federal Democratic Republic of Nepal

Capital City: Kathmandu

Nepal is a landlocked country in South Asia. It has a total area of 147,181 km2, with a population of 28,850,717 as of 2016. Its economy is based on tourism, handicrafts, garments, carpets, tea, coffee, IT services, and hydropower. Swayambhunath (image above), is the second most important shrine in Kathmandu, Nepal. It sits atop of a hill where many monkeys live. And so, the temple is more affectionately known as the Monkey Temple. Originally a prehistoric cult site, the temple is now a sacred place for the Vajrayana Buddhists of Northern Nepal and Tibet, and for the Newari Buddhists of the Kathmandu Valley.

Netherlands

Official Name: Kingdom of the Netherlands

Capital City: Amsterdam

Netherlands is a small country in Western Europe. It is bordered by Germany, Belgium and the North Sea. It has an area of 41,543 km2 and a population of 16,979,729. In the United Nations World Happiness 2013 Report, the country ranked as the seventh-happiest country in the world. The country's capital, Amsterdam (image above), is considered as one of Europe's most popular tourist destinations. It has more than 1500 fabulous monumental building, as well as bridges and museums near the canals across the city.

New Zealand

Official Name: New Zealand

Capital City: Wellington

New Zealand is an island nation in the southwestern Pacific Ocean. It is about 268,021 km2 in size, with around 4,565,185 residents. The country is also considered a high-income economy, with high rankings in health, education, economic freedom and quality of life. Champagne Pool (image above), is a prominent geothermal feature in New Zealand. The hot spring had its name derived from the abundant efflux in its surface or flowing out of carbon dioxide gas which looks like a glass of bubbling champagne. Formed 900 years ago the spring is around 65 meters in diameter with a maximum depth of about 62 meters.

Nicaragua

Official Name: Republic of Nicaragua

Capital City: Managua

Nicaragua is the largest country in the Central American isthmus (a narrow strip of land with sea on either side), with its 130,375 km2 territory. On the other hand, its capital city, Managua is regarded as the third-largest city in Central America. As of 2016, the population in the country is around 6,150,035. Cerro Negro (image above), is a young and active volcano, where tourists frequently visit, for volcano boarding – a famous activity in the black volcano. The activity starts with a hike to the top which takes around an hour, there the tourist will sit on a piece of wood, and then slide down side of the volcano.

Niger

Official Name: Republic of Niger

Capital City: Niamey

Niger is another landlocked country in Western Africa. It covers a land area of 1,267,000 km2, making it the largest country in West Africa. More than 80 percent of its territory is covered by the Sahara Desert. Its population, on the other hand was estimated around 17,138,707. Kouré (image above), is a rural community in Niger. It is where the last herd of West African giraffes, an endemic type of giraffe in West Africa can be found. The population of these particular giraffes is around 170 only.

Nigeria

Official Name: Federal Republic of Nigeria

Capital City: Abuja

Nigeria is a nation located in West Africa and bordered by Benin, Chad, Cameroon and Niger. Its territory is 923,768 km2 in size, while the inhabitants are around 186,987,563 people. Today, the country is a home to numerous kingdoms and tribal states. One of the most notable attractions in Nigeria is the Zuma Rock (image above) – a large monolith or single upright block of stone. It rises spectacularly immediately north of Nigeria's capital Abuja, and is sometimes referred to as the "Gateway to Abuja". It was once used for a defensive retreat by the ethnic group called, Gbagyi people against invading neighboring tribes during intertribal warring.

North Korea

Official Name: Democratic People's Republic of Korea

Capital City: Pyongyang

North Korea is a country in East Asia bordered by China, Russia, Tumen rivers and South Korea. It is about 120,540 km2 in size and has a population of 25,281,327. It also has active duty army of 1.21 million – the fourth largest army in the world. The Juche Tower (image above), is one of Pyongyang's monuments. From the top of the Juche Tower one can have a panoramic view of the entire city. One can also simply sit at the steps of the tower in a laid back manner and watch the residents of the capital getting along with their daily lives.

Norway

Official Name: Kingdom of Norway

Capital City: Oslo

Norway is a nation which is about 385,178 km2 in size. As of 206, the estimated population in the country is 5,271,958 people. Outside the Middle East, the country is one of the world's largest producers of oil and natural gas. Jotunheimen, or Home of the Giants (image above), is Norway's national park that encompasses several mountain ranges. There are lodges and well-marked trails in these mountains that offer visitors easy access to glacier hikes, summit tours, mountain climbing and skiing.

Oman

Official Name: Sultanate of Oman

Capital City: Muscat

Oman is an Arab country located at the mouth of the Persian Gulf. It is bordered by United Arab Emirates, Saudi Arabia, Yemen and the Arabian Sea. It has about 4,654,471 inhabitants in its 309,500 km2 territory. Aside from its oil reserves, the country's economy also includes tourism and trade of fish, dates, and certain agricultural produce. The Taqah Castle (image above), which dates back from the 19th century is one of the tourist destinations in Oman. It was built to be the permanent residence of Sheikh Ali bin Al Ma'shani Timman, the second wife of Sultan Said bin Taimur (sultan of Muscat and Oman from February 10, 1932 to July 23, 1970 and the mother of Qaboos bin Said al Said (Sultan of Oman from July 23, 1970 up to present).

Pakistan

Official Name: Islamic Republic of Pakistan

Capital City: Islamabad

Pakistan is a country in South Asia bordered by India, Afghanistan, Iran and China. It has 192,826,502 residents, making it the sixth-most populous country in the world. It is also noted as the 36th largest country in the world with its 881,913 km2 total area. One of the attractions in Pakistan is the Pakistan Monument (image above). It was opened on March 23, 2007 as a national monument embodying the country's history. Its design was inspired by the figure of a blossoming flower to represent the four provinces and three territories into which Pakistan is subdivided. The structure itself is made up of four bigger 'petals' (the provinces), alternated with three smaller ones (the territories). When viewed from above, it represents the five-pointed star on Pakistan's national flag.

Palau

Official Name: Republic of Palau

Capital City: Ngerulmud

Palau is an island country in the western Pacific Ocean made up of around 250 islands. It has a population of 21,501 on its 465.55 km2 territory. Its economy is dependent on tourism, agriculture and fishing. One of the must-see places in the country is the Palau International Coral Reef Center (image above). It is the ideal spot for children and family to enjoy aquarium that offers educational exhibits about life in the coral reef and conservation practices for reef systems.

Palestine

Official Name: State of Palestine

Capital City: East Jerusalem

Palestine is a state in the Middle East. It covers a territory of 6,220 km2 and has approximately 4,797,239 inhabitants. Its independence was declared on November 15, 1988. Abraham Mosque (image above), which is found in Palestine is the fourth holiest place for Muslims. Based on Arabian legends, the huge stone of the walls is set up by the prophet Solomon, with the help of the genies.

Panama

Official Name: Republic of Panama

Capital City: Panama City

Panama is a country located between North America and South America. It has 3,990,406 residents, nearly half of which lives in the country's capital and largest city – Panama City. The San Blas Islands (image above), which is located in Panama is the best place to explore the rich culture of the country's indigenous people – the Kuna. The Kuna people treat this place as their own. In fact, one member of the tribe is stationed on many of the area's tiny tropical islands. For a nominal fee, they allow visitors exclusive use of the island for the day.

Papua New Guinea

Official Name: Independent State of Papua New Guinea

Capital City: Port Moresby

Papua New Guinea is a country that occupies a 462,840 km2 territory. Its population in 2016 is around 7,776,115, only 18 percent of which live in urban areas. It is also considered as one of the world's least explored country, with many undiscovered types of plants and animals, as well as groups of uncontacted people. Despite being the tallest mountain in Papua New Guinea, Mount Wilhelm (image above) is an accessible and 'climbable' mountain. Hikes to the top of the mountain last between three to four days. The duration depends on the route taken and the level of experience of the climber.

Paraguay

Official Name: Republic of Paraguay

Capital City: Asuncion

Paraguay is a landlocked country bordered by Argentina, Brazil and Bolivia. It is often referred to as Corazón de Sudamérica, which means, "Heart of South America" due to its central location in South America. The country also has 406,752 km2 territory and 6,725,430 population. Asuncion (image above), is one of the oldest city in Paraguay and even in South America. For the children, they can enjoy many activities in the botanical gardens and the zoo in this city. Adults, on the other hand, can spend their time wandering through the city's museums and charming historical district.

Peru

Official Name: Republic of Peru

Capital City: Lima

Peru is a country in South America and is bordered by Ecuador, Colombia, Brazil Bolivia, Chile and the Pacific Ocean. It covers an area of 1,285,216 km2, where approximately 31,774,225 people live. The Sacred Valley of the Incas (image above), is a valley in Peru. It was once the heartland of the Inca Empire – the largest empire in Pre-Columbian era (before 1942). It contains numerous archaeological remains and villages including the Inca cities of Písac and Ollantaytambo.

Philippines

Official Name: Republic of the Philippines

Capital City: Manila

The Philippines is an island country in Southeast Asia. It has about 7,641 islands which covers a total area of 300,000 km2. Located close to the equator, the country is prone to earthquakes and typhoons. However, it is also blessed with abundant natural resources. As of 2016, the population in the country is around 102,250,133 people. Puerto Princesa, which is located in the Philippines, is a nature lover's paradise. It is home to one of the world's most unique natural phenomena – the underground river (image above). Also known as the Puerto Princesa Subterranean River, this natural wonder is the world's longest navigable underground river. Tours in this amazing spot show intriguing rock formations and fluttering bats.

Poland

Official Name: Republic of Poland

Capital City: Warsaw

Poland is a country located in Central Europe with a total area of 312,679 km2, making it the 9th largest country in Europe. With a population of 38,593,161 people, the country is also noted as the 8th most populous country in Europe. The medieval town of Malbork or Marienburg is a major tourist destination found in Poland. It is famous for its castle (image above), which was built in the 13th century for 230 years by the Knights of the Teutonic Order as their headquarters. It is named after the Virgin Mary, the patron saint of the city and castle. This particular castle is actually made up of three castles, making it the world's largest brick castle. Many parts of the castle were destroyed during World War II. However, the castle has been restored since then.

Portugal

Official Name: Portuguese Republic

Capital City: Lisbon

Portugal is a country in Southwestern Europe bordered by the Atlantic Ocean and Spain. It has a 92,212 km2 total area and a population of 10,304,434. Considered as a well-developed country, Portugal has a high-income advanced economy and high living standards. Aveiro (image above), a city in Portugal often referred to as "the Venice of Portugal", is a picturesque area with scenic canals connected by charming bridges. Colorful gondolas and speed boats can be found in these canals to offer transportation. Aside from gorgeous views, the city is also popular for its tasty cuisine.

Qatar

Official Name: State of Qatar

Capital City: Doha

Qatar is a country in Southwest Asia bordered by Saudi Arabia and by the Persian Gulf. It covers an area of 11,586 km2 where approximately 2,291,368 people live. The country is regarded as a high income economy due to its vast natural gas reserves and oil reserves which are the third largest in the world. The Museum of Islamic Art (image above), is a tourist destination in Qatar that is the perfect example of how beautiful Islamic art is. With its very modern architecture, it was fully ready to accommodate tourists. Inside is a huge collection of Muslim world art, including the Arab, Persian and Africa. There are also art exhibitions found inside, starting from the plastic art to the Clothes of Muslim world.

Romania

Official Name: Romania

Capital City: Bucharest

Romania is a state in Southeast Europe which covers a territory of 238,391 km2. It is bordered by the Black Sea, Bulgaria, Ukraine, Hungary, Serbia, and Moldova. Its population is around 19,372,734, making it the seventh most populous member state of the European Union. One of the most beautiful places in Romania is Sinaia – a mountain resort town in Romania. King Charles I built his summer home in this town. The summer home is known as Peles Castle (image above) – a popular tourist attraction.

Russia

Official Name: Russian Federation

Capital City: Moscow

Russia is a state in northern Eurasia. Occupying a total area of 17,075,200 km2, it is considered as the largest country in the world. With a population of 143,439,832, the country is also regarded as the ninth most populous. Lake Baikal (image above), is one of the top tourist destinations in Russia. It is considered as the deepest and oldest lake on Earth. This 25-million-year-old lake is surrounded by mountain ranges and is also noted as one of the clearest lakes in the world.

Rwanda

Official Name: Republic of Rwanda

Capital City: Kigali

Rwanda is a state in central and east Africa. With its 26,338 km2 total area, it is regarded as one of the smallest countries in the mainland of Africa. As of July 2016, the country has an estimated population of 11,882,766 people. The Ethnographic Museum or the National Museum of Rwanda (image above), is one of the most famous destinations in Rwanda. It first opened in 1989 and contains ethnographic collections or documentations about the cultural history of the country.

Saint Kitts and Nevis

Official Name: Federation of Saint Kitts and Nevis

Capital City: Basseterre

The Saint Kitts and Nevis is a two-island country located in the West Indies. It has a territory of just 261 km2 and a population of only 56,183 people. It is also sometimes referred to as "The Mother Colony of the West Indies" as this country was home to the first British and French colonies in the Caribbean. The Brimstone Hill Fortress (image above) is one of the 'must-visit' places in Saint Kitts and Nevis. It was built in 1690 by African slaves to defend the country against invaders. It now houses a museum and is considered as a Unesco world heritage site.

Saint Lucia

Official Name: Saint Lucia

Capital City: Castries

Saint Lucia is an island country located in the Caribbean Sea. It covers a land area of 617 km2 and has a population of 186,383, as of 2016. Before, this country was rules by either French or British. And because of the often switched in control between British and French control, Saint Lucia was also known as the "Helen of the West Indies". One of the most beautiful places in Saint Lucia is the Diamond Falls (image above). This beautiful waterfall is regarded as the most colorful waterfall in the Caribbean. Its waters were laced with minerals as its stream originating from rainwater mixed with volcanic discharges giving the falls a rather colorful appearance that seemed to change often.

Saint Vincent and the Grenadines

Official Name: Saint Vincent and the Grenadines

Capital City: Kingstown

Saint Vincent and the Grenadines is an island country in the Caribbean Sea. Its 389 km2 territory mostly lies within the Hurricane Belt, an area in the Atlantic Ocean which is likely to get hurricanes. As of 2016, the population in the country is around 109,644. Mustique a privately owned island is a playground for celebrities, rock stars, and the uber-rich. It has its own airport, general store, luxury hotels and private villas. It offers excellent opportunities for swimming and snorkeling. Macaroni Beach (image above), is a favorite area in the island.

Samoa

Official Name: Independent State of Samoa

Capital City: Apia

Samoa is a state which is 2,842 km2 in size. As of July, 2016, it has around 194,523 inhabitants. Due to Samoans' seafaring skills, this country was referred to as "Navigator Islands". The blowholes (image above) near Taga village in Samoa are truly powerful. They propel roaring jets of water hundreds of feet up into the air. These are particularly worth watching when locals throw coconuts into the holes which are blasted into the air.

San Marino

Official Name: Republic of San Marino

Capital City: City of San Marino

San Marino is a microstate surrounded by Italy. It has a territory just 61.2 km2 and has an estimated population (in 2016) of 31,950. Founded on September 3, 301 this country was claimed to be the oldest surviving sovereign state in the world. It also was regarded to have the earliest written constitution which is still in effect. The Palazzo Pubblico (image above) is the town hall of the City of San Marino. This is the building where official State ceremonies take place. The main section of the building is topped by battlements or regularly spaced, squared openings. The clock tower above also features such an arrangement with battlements and corbels. Overall, the design of this structure is similar to the Palazzo Vecchio, the town hall of Florence, Italy.

Sao Tome and Principe

Official Name: Democratic Republic of São Tomé and Príncipe

Capital City: São Tomé

São Tomé and Príncipe is an island nation located in the Gulf of Guinea. It has a population of just 194,390 people and an area of only 964 km2, making it the second-smallest African country. The highest mountain on the islands, Pico Cão Grande (image above), is about 6,800 feet high. It is located in the center of São Tomé Island, and is covered in thick forest, making it great for hiking and trekking. The forested areas in this mountain are home to many different kinds of plants and animals.

Saudi Arabia

Official Name: Kingdom of Saudi Arabia

Capital City: Riyadh

Saudi Arabia is an Arab state which is 2,149,690 km2 in size, making it the fifth-largest state in Asia. As of 2016, the residents in the country are around 32,157,974. Since 1938, this country has since become the world's largest oil producer and exporter, with its oil reserves (second largest in the world) and gas reserves (sixth largest). One of the major attractions in Saudi Arabia is the King Fahd's Fountain. It is one of the best places in the country and is extremely fascinating as it is the world's tallest fountain in the city of Jeddah. Located at the red sea, it propels salty sea water to the height of 853 meters. The night illumination looks like as if the angels are coming down on earth.

Senegal

Official Name: Republic of Senegal

Capital City: Dakar

Senegal is a country in West Africa bordered by Mauritania, Mali, Guinea and Guinea-Bissau. It has around 15,589,485 people in its 196,712 km2 territory. Its economical and political capital city is called Dakar. One of the most interesting places in Senegal is the Retba Lake, or Pink Lake (image above). It has an incredible pink-purple color due to its high salt content, unique bacteria, and the reflection of sunlight. Visitors in this lake can also view the salt harvesting that takes place – an important agricultural industry for the country.

Serbia

Official Name: Republic of Serbia

Capital City: Belgrade

Serbia is a landlocked state located in Europe bordered by Hungary, Romania, Bulgaria, Macedonia, Croatia, Bosnia, and Montenegro. It has a territory of about 88,361 km2 and a population of around 8,812,705. One of the 'must-see' places in Serbia is the Đavolja Varoš or Devil's Town (image above). It features 202 exotic rock formations described as earth pyramids or "towers". These towers are around 2-15 meters tall and 4-6 meters wide at the base. These formations were created by strong erosion of the soil due to intense volcanic activity millions of years ago.

Seychelles

Official Name: Republic of Seychelles

Capital City: Victoria

Seychelles is a country found in the Indian Ocean. It is made up of 115 islands covering a total area of 459 km2. With a population of just 97,026, this particular country is noted for having the smallest population of any independent African state. Anse Lazio (image above) is one of Seychelles' most picturesque beaches. It features rounded granite boulders, blond sand and crystal clear waters in dreamy shades of blue. The shallow area of the beach is an excellent place for swimming and snorkeling.

Sierra Leone

Official Name: Republic of Sierra Leone

Capital City: Freetown

Sierra Leone is a country in West Africa bordered by Guinea, Liberia, and the Atlantic Ocean. It has a total area of 71,740 km2 and an estimated population of 6,592,102, as per United Nation's 2016 estimation. The country's economy was dependent on mining – diamonds, titanium, gold and rutile. Mount Bintumani or Loma Mansa (image above), is the highest peak in Sierra Leone. It is about 1,945 meters tall. Its lower slopes are covered in rainforests, which is home to a wide variety of animals including: pygmy hippopotamuses, dwarf crocodiles, rufous fishing-owls and numerous primates.

Singapore

Official Name: Republic of Singapore

Capital City: Singapore

Singapore, which is also known as the Lion City, the Garden City and the Red Dot, is a state in Southeast Asia. It is the world's only island city-state. It is about 719.1 km2 in size and has 5,696,506 inhabitants. One of the best places in Singapore is the Gardens by the Bay (image above), a nature park which is about 101 hectares in size. This beautiful garden is part of a strategy by the Singapore government to transform the state from a "Garden City" to a "City in a Garden". The aim of this project is to raise the quality of life by enhancing greenery and flora (plants) in the city.

Slovakia

Official Name: Slovak Republic

Capital City: Bratislava

Slovakia is a landlocked country in Central Europe bordered by Czech Republic, Austria, Poland, Ukraine and Hungary. Its territory is about 49,035 km2, most of which is mountainous. The population, on the other hand is 5,429,418. One of the highly-visited places in Slovakia is the Carpathian Wooden Churches (image above). It is a UNESCO World Heritage Site that has nine wooden religious buildings constructed between the 16th and 18th centuries. These wooden churches include two Roman Catholic churches, three Protestant churches, three Greek Catholic churches and one belfry or bell tower that are located in different places in Slovakia.

Slovenia

Official Name: Republic of Slovenia

Capital City: Ljubljana

Slovenia is a state located in Central Europe. This 20,273 km2 state is bordered by Italy, Austria, Hungary, Croatia and the Adriatic Sea. As of July, 2016, the estimated population in the state is 2,069,362 people. Bled (image above), is a fairy tale-like city and is Slovenia's spot for best resorts. It features a picturesque lake and a magnificent looking Bled Castle. This nice town is great for travelers who love canoeing, hiking and cycling.

Solomon Islands

Official Name: Solomon Islands

Capital City: Honiara

Solomon Islands is a country made up of six major islands and more than 900 smaller islands in Oceania. It covers an area of 28,400 km2 and has a population of approximately 594,934. Marovo Lagoon (image above), is one of the Solomon Islands' most spectacular attractions. It is home to amazing kinds of bird. This salt-water lagoon is also perfect for diving. Aside from diving, visitors can also sit back, relax and enjoy the surrounding beauty of Marovo Lagoon.

Somalia

Official Name: Federal Republic of Somalia

Capital City: Mogadishu

Somalia is a country in the Horn of Africa bordered by Ethiopia, Djibouti, the Gulf of Aden, the Indian Ocean and Kenya. It covers an area of 637,657 km2, while the estimated population is approximately 11,079,013 people. The best-known landmark in Somalia is Laas Geel (image above). It is a series of caves that display hundreds of ancient Neolithic paintings. The rock art in these caves dating back to 9000 BC is one of the best-preserved anywhere in the world.

South Africa

Official Name: Republic of South Africa

Capital City: Pretoria

South Africa is the southernmost state in Africa. With its 1,221,037 km2 territory and 54,978,907 inhabitants, this country is considered as the world's 24th-most populous nation. Today the country is a developed and a newly industrialized country with upper-middle-income economy. South Africa's second-largest city, Durban (image above), is a popular vacation destination as its scenic beaches is close to Johannesburg, one of the modern cities in the country.

South Korea

Official Name: Republic of Korea

Capital City: Seoul

South Korea is a state in East Asia just south of North Korea. This highly urbanized and mountainous country covers a territory of 100,210 km2. It has a population of 50,503,933, about half of which live in the capital city, Seoul. Gyeongbokgung Palace (image above) in South Korea is arguably the most beautiful and grandest of all five palaces in the country. Its name means, "Palace of Shining Happiness". Once destroyed by fire at the time of Japanese occupation from 1592-1598, the palace is now fully restored.

South Sudan

Official Name: Republic of South Sudan

Capital City: Juba

South Sudan is another landlocked country in Africa bordered by Sudan, Ethiopia, Kenya, Uganda, the Democratic Republic of the Congo and the Central African Republic. It is about 619,745 km2 in size and has 12,733,427 residents. The longest river in the world, the Nile River (image above), passes through South Sudan and is now the dominant geographic attraction of the country. There are many bars and restaurants in the country one can visit that will give a beautiful scenic view of the White Nile River.

Spain

Official Name: Kingdom of Spain

Capital City: Madrid

Spain is a state largely located in Europe. It covers a total area of 505,990 km2 and has a population around 46,064,604 people. Its official language is Spanish – the world's second most spoken first language. It is also a developed country with the world's fourteenth largest economy. The Basílica i Temple Expiatori de la Sagrada Família (image above), is a large Roman Catholic church in Barcelona, Spain. Although incomplete, the church is a UNESCO World Heritage Site. In November 2010, Pope Benedict XVI proclaimed this church as a minor basilica.

Sri Lanka

Official Name: Democratic Socialist Republic of Sri Lanka

Capital City: Sri Jayawardenepura Kotte

Sri Lanka is an island country in South Asia near south-east India. It has about 20,810,816 inhabitants spread throughout its 65,610 km2 territory. Polonnaruwa (image above), is where one will find Sri Lanka's finest collection of ancient Buddhist art and architecture. It includes magnificent rock-carved statues and the exquisitely decorated temples of the Quadrangle.

Sudan

Official Name: Republic of the Sudan

Capital City: Khartoum

Sudan is a country in Africa bordered by Egypt, the Red Sea, Eritrea, Ethiopia, South Sudan, Central African Republic, Chad and Libya. With its 1,886,068 km2 total area, it is noted as the third largest country in Africa. When it comes to population, the country has 41,175,541 residents as of 2016. By far, the most popular tourist destination in Sudan is the Pyramids of Meroe (image above).It is noted as one of the last remaining symbols from an ancient civilization. It was built by the Meroitic Pharaohs around 500 BC. Different from the pyramids in Egypt, Pyramids of Meroe features steep brick sides and appear in groups of 12. Travelers are permitted to enter the pyramids, in which ancient graffiti and hieroglyphics can be seen.

Suriname

Official Name: Republic of Suriname

Capital City: Paramaribo

Suriname is a state in South America and is bordered by French Guiana, Guyana and Brazil. With its 163,821 km2 total area, it is regarded as the smallest country in South America. It also has a population of 547,610 most of whom live on the country's north coast. Brokopondo Reservoir (image above), is a storage space for water. It is considered as one of the largest reservoirs in the world. It provides a much-needed boost to the aluminum industry, as well as fishing opportunities. A man-made beauty, the Brokopondo Reservoir is a tourist destination in itself.

Swaziland

Official Name: Kingdom of Swaziland

Capital City: Lobamba

Swaziland is a state in Southern Africa near Mozambique and South Africa. With its 17,364 km2 territory, it is one of the smallest countries in Africa. As of 2016, the population in the country reaches about 1,304,063. In addition, the country is also a developing country with a small economy and is classified as a country with a lower-middle income. The Shewula Mountain Camp (image above) was Swaziland's first community-owned eco-tourism attraction. It offers amazing views and a different kind of tourism where visitors can partake in village walks to get to know the local community and its members. Visitors can also witness traditional song and dance performances, visit a traditional healer, or just enjoy the tranquil natural surroundings.

Sweden

Official Name: Kingdom of Sweden

Capital City: Stockholm

Sweden is a country in Northern Europe bordered by Norway, Finland and Denmark. It has a total area of 450,295 km2, with a total population of 9,851,852. Today, the country has the world's eighth-highest income and ranks highly in quality of life, health, education, prosperity, economic competitiveness, equality and human development. The Vasa Museum in Stockholm, Sweden is the most popular museum in the country. More than 20 million people have visited since the museum opened in 1990, as people want to see the Vasa (image above) – a battle ship that sank on its first voyage. Lying below the icy waters for more than 300 years, an ambitious salvage operation took place. Now, this fascinating old battle ship attracts millions of tourists every year.

Switzerland

Official Name: Swiss Confederation

Capital City: Bern

Switzerland is a landlocked country in Europe bordered by Italy, France, Germany, Austria and Liechtenstein. It is about 41,285 km2 in size, with Alps (a mountain rang) occupying the greater part of the territory. As of 2016, its population is around 8,379,477. Lucerne in Switzerland is considered one of the world's prettiest cities. It is most famous for its 14th century Chapel Bridge (image above) and Water Tower, which is said to be the most photographed monument in Switzerland. The Chapel Bridge is a covered wooden footbridge placed diagonally across the Reuss River. Its name was derived from the nearby St. Peter's Chapel.

Syria

Official Name: Syrian Arab Republic

Capital City: Damascus

Syria is a country in Western Asia bordered by Lebanon, the Mediterranean Sea, Turkey, Iraq, Jordan and Israel. Its total area is about 185,180 km2 in size, with approximately 18,563,595 residents. The Shrine of John the Baptist (image above), is an interesting place to visit in Syria. The local legend says that during the building of the Umayyad Mosque in the 8th century, a casket was found at the site. Inside the casket was John The Baptist's head – complete with his hair and skin. On the spot where they discovered it, they built the shrine, which is a green dome-shaped structure. Although the authenticity of this story and the person in the shrine is disputed, the shrine still remains a very popular destination for tourists.

Taiwan

Official Name: Republic of China

Capital City: Taipei

Taiwan is a state in East Asia which is not a member of the United Nations. It has an area of 36,193 km2 and a population of 23,395,600 people. It is one of the Four Asian Tigers or Asian Dragons, made up of the highly developed economies of Hong Kong, Singapore, South Korea and Taiwan. Taipei 101 (image above), which was formerly known as the Taipei World Financial Center, is a super tall skyscraper in Taipei, Taiwan. This building was officially classified as the world's tallest in 2004 until 2009. With 101 floors, the construction if this tower started in 1999 and finished in 2004 and has served as an icon of modern Taiwan ever since its opening. It was also created as a symbol of the evolution of technology and Asian tradition.

Tajikistan

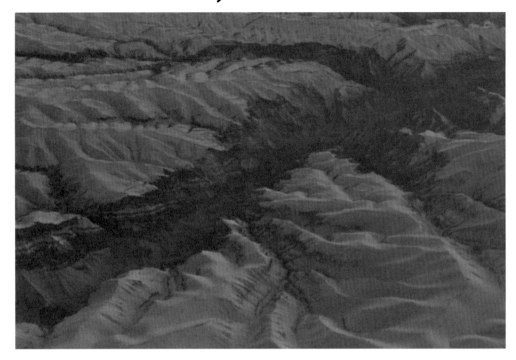

Official Name: Republic of Tajikistan

Capital City: Dushanbe

143,100 km2

Tajikistan is another landlocked country in Central Asia. It has an estimated 8,669,464 people in 2016. It covers an area of 143,100 km2, more than 90% of which is covered by mountains. The Pamir Mountains (image above), are a great destination spot in Tajikistan. The activities that can be done around this mountain range includes, horse riding, rock climbing and many others. One may also encounter some sheep herders in the upper meadowlands.

Tanzania

Official Name: United Republic of Tanzania

Capital City: Dodoma

Tanzania is a large country in Eastern Africa. It is about 947,303 km2 in size where an estimated 55,155,473 people live. Its capital city is Dodoma, where the President's Office, the National Assembly, and some government ministries are located. One of the most beautiful attractions in Tanzania is Mount Kilimanjaro National Park (image above). It is Africa's highest mountain peak. It is visited by tourists for the chance to stand in awe of this majestic snow-capped mountain and to climb to the summit. Mount Kilimanjaro can be climbed at any time, although the best period is from late June to October, during the dry season.

Thailand

Official Name: Kingdom of Thailand

Capital City: Bangkok

Thailand, which is formerly known as Siam is a country in Southeast Asia. It covers an area of 513,120 km2. As of July, 2016, its population was estimated to be around 68,146,609, making it the 20th-most-populous country in the world. The city of Ayuthaya (image above) in Thailand was once the capital of the Ayuthaya Kingdom, or Siam. It was also once declared as the most magnificent city on earth, with three palaces, more than 400 temples and a population that reached nearly 1,000,000. However, in 1767, the Burmese attacked and conquered Ayuthaya. The ruins of Ayuthaya are now a major attraction for those visiting Thailand.

Togo

Official Name: Togolese Republic

Capital City: Lome

Togo is a country in West Africa which is 56,785 km2 in size —one of the smallest countries in Africa. It is bordered by Ghana, Benin and Burkina Faso. As of 2016, its population is around 7,496,833 people. Lake Togo (image above) is one of the most important places in Togo. It is considered as the center of voodoo culture a belief system or spiritual folkway that started in West Africa. In addition, the lake itself offers plentiful boating opportunities. It is also shallow and a popular location for water sports.

Tonga

Official Name: Kingdom of Tonga

Capital City: Nuku'alofa

Tonga is a state made up of 169 islands, only 36 of which are inhabited. It only has a 748 km2 land area spread over 700,000 square km2 of the southern Pacific Ocean. Its population is 106,915 as of 2016. One of the must-see places in Tonga is the Mapu a Vaea or "Whistle of the Noble" (image above). These are natural blowholes on the island of Tongatapu. When waves crash into the reef, natural channels in the volcanic rock allow water to forcefully blow through and propel into the air. Witnessing these blowholes is considered as one of the highlights of the tours around the island of Tongatapu.

Trinidad and Tobago

Official Name: Republic of Trinidad and Tobago

Capital City: Port of Spain

Trinidad and Tobago is a twin island country that is located in South America. Its territory covers an area of 5,131 km2. As of July 2016, the estimated population in the country is around 1,364,973 people. This nation is regarded as a rich country. It also has a developed and high income economy. One of the most popular tourist destinations in Trinidad and Tobago is the Maracas Bay (image above). It became a very famous beach in the country due to its golden sand and close proximity to the city.

Tunisia

Official Name: Tunisia

Capital City: Tunis

Tunisia is the northernmost country in Africa bordered by Algeria, Libya, and the Mediterranean Sea. It covers an area of 163,610 km2 and a population around 11,375,220. One of the best places in Tunisia is the Sidi Bou Said (image above), a cliff-top village with whitewashed alleyways, iron window frames and blue doors. This Tunisian village is noted as architecture at its finest. It also offers a fantastic view of the sea.

Turkey

Official Name: Republic of Turkey

Capital City: Ankara

Turkey is a country with territories lying in Western Asia and in Southeast Europe. It is about 783,356 km2 in size. As of 2016, its population is around 79,622,062, 85% of whom speaks Turkish, the country's official language. One of the most interesting destinations in Turkey is the Cappadocia (image above). It is best known for its fairytale landscape of unusual rock formations resembling chimneys, cones and pinnacles. Volcanic eruptions and erosion that happened million years ago have all resulted to these odd formations. Thousands of years ago, mankind carved out houses, churches and underground cities from the soft rocks. Underground tunnels were also built in this area to escape invaders. Today, some of the caves in the region are actually hotels and cater to tourists.

Turkmenistan

Official Name: Turkmenistan

Capital City: Ashgabat

Turkmenistan is a country in Central Asia about 491,210 km2 in size. As of July, 2016, its residents are approximately 5,438,670 people. When it comes to economy, this country has the world's fourth largest natural gas reserves that in 1993, citizens in the country received free electricity, water and natural gas from the government. In addition, most of the Turkmenistan is covered by the Karakum Desert. Merv (image above), is a town in Turkmenistan. It was said to be the largest city in the world around the 12th Century. It is also believed that the Hindu religion started here in Mount Meru which Hinduism declares to be the center of the world.

Tuvalu

Official Name: Tuvalu

Capital City: Funafuti

Tuvalu, which was formerly known as the Ellice Islands is an island nation in the Pacific Ocean. It has a population of only 9,943 as of 2016. The total land area of the islands is just 26 km2. Funafuti (image above) is an atoll or ring-shaped reef, island considered as the capital of Tuvalu. It has a population of over six thousand people, making it the most populated atoll. It encircles a large lagoon, which is by far, the largest lagoon in Tuvalu. This lagoon is about 14 kilometers wide and 18 kilometers long and is excellent for swimming and snorkeling.

Uganda

Official Name: Republic of Uganda

Capital City: Kampala

Uganda is a 241,038 km2 landlocked country bordered to the east by Kenya, South Sudan, Democratic Republic of the Congo, Rwanda and Tanzania. With a population of 40,322,768, this country was regarded as the world's second most populous landlocked country. One of the most visited places in Uganda is the Kasubi Tombs (image above) –the burial site of the four kings of the Kingdom of Buganda (a kingdom within Uganda). In 2010 many of the buildings were destroyed by a fire. However, the Government is committed to restoring the tombs as soon as possible.

Ukraine

Official Name: Ukraine

Capital City: Kiev

Ukraine is a state in Eastern Europe about 603,500 km2 in size, making it the largest country in Europe. It is also noted as the 32nd most populous country in the world with its 44,624,373 inhabitants. Lviv (image above), is a city in Ukraine which was used to be part of Poland until after the World War II. It is regarded as one of the main cultural hubs of Ukraine and is known for world-famous ballet, opera and orchestra. It is a beautiful city with cobbled streets and fabulous architecture.

United Arab Emirates

Official Name: United Arab Emirates

Capital City: Abu Dhabi

United Arab Emirates or the Emirates, or the UAE is a country in the Arabian Peninsula. It is about 83,600 km2 in size. It is bordered by Oman and Saudi Arabia. In 2016, the country's estimated population was 9,266,971. Burj Khalifa (image above), is a famous landmark in Dubai, UAE. At 829.8 meters, it is the tallest building in the world. On the 124th floor, there is an observation deck here that offers an excellent view of the desert on one side and the ocean on the other. Night-time visits are also popular due to Dubai's famous city-lights panoramas.

United Kingdom

Official Name: United Kingdom of Great Britain and Northern Ireland

Capital City: London

United Kingdom or Britain is a state in Europe surrounded by the Atlantic Ocean. With an area of 242,495 km2, it is regarded as the 11th-largest state in Europe. It is also considered as the 22nd-most populous country, with its population of approximately 65,111,143. One of the most famous sites in the world which is located in UK is the Stonehenge (image above). It is made up of large standing stones arrange in a ring pattern. It was believed to be constructed thousands of years ago. There are no written records about the Stonehenge as to how it was built and for what purpose. However, there are many theories that have been proposed as to why it was built. One of the theories said that the Stonehenge was used as a place of healing. Another theory states that this site served as a burial ground and a place for worship.

United States of America

Official Name: United States of America

Capital City: Washington, D.C.

The United States of America (USA), which is also called the United States (U.S.) or America, is a country that covers an area of 9,833,517 km2 – the world's third largest country. Its population of about 324,118,787 also makes the country the third most populous in the world. The Grand Canyon (image above) is one of the best places to visit in the USA. It can be found in Arizona, USA. This massive natural wonder was carved by the Colorado River over a period of several million years. It is neither the deepest nor the longest canyon in the world. However, its overwhelming size and colorful landscape offers visitors breathtaking views that are hard to match.

Uruguay

Official Name: Oriental Republic of Uruguay

Capital City: Montevideo

Uruguay is a country in South America bordered by Argentina, Brazil, the Río de la Plata (River of Silver) and the Atlantic Ocean. It has a population of 3,444,071 and a total area of 176,215 km2, making it the second-smallest nation in South America. Colonia del Sacramento (image above), is a top destination in Uruguay due to its closeness to its famous neighbor, Buenos Aires, the capital of Argentina. However, what makes this region so popular is its ancient cobbled streets lined with museums, churches and old buildings.

Uzbekistan

Official Name: Republic of Uzbekistan

Capital City: Tashkent

Uzbekistan is a landlocked country in Central Asia bordered by Kazakhstan, Tajikistan, Kyrgyzstan, Afghanistan and Turkmenistan. Its 448,978 km2 territory is home to approximately 30,300,446 people. Its economy is highly dependent on cotton, gold, uranium and natural gas. Khiva (image above), is a fascinating Uzbekistan town. This hardly inhabited town is well preserved as it still lies in its original walls, having changed very little since it was constructed in early 18th century.

Vanuatu

Official Name: Republic of Vanuatu

Capital City: Port Vila

Vanuatu is an island nation in the South Pacific Ocean. It is about 12,189 km2 in size with an estimated population of just 270,470. Formerly claimed by France and Great Britain, the country became independent in 1980. The Nanda Blue Hole (image above) is often regarded by visitors as the most beautiful blue hole in Vanuatu. The water here has a magical deep blue color. This amazing natural creation was formed by springs of fresh pure water rising to the surface cutting out a deep hole in the limestone surface.

Vatican City

Official Name: Vatican City State or State of Vatican City

Capital City: Vatican City

Vatican City is a walled enclave or portion of a territory within the city of Rome. It has an area of just 0.44 km2 and a population of only 801 people, making it the smallest state in the world when it comes to area and population. This state is being ruled by the Bishop of Rome or the Pope. The Papal Basilica of St. Peter in the Vatican, or simply St. Peter's Basilica (image above), is an important destination in the city. This Italian Renaissance church is the most renowned work and one of the largest churches in the world. It is also regarded as one of the holiest Catholic shrines. According to Catholic tradition it is the burial site of St. Peter, one of Christ's Apostles and also the first Pope, with the tomb directly below the high altar of the Basilica.

Venezuela

Official Name: Bolivarian Republic of Venezuela

Capital City: Caracas

Venezuela is country in South America bordered by Colombia, Brazil, Guyana and Trinidad and Tobago. Its territory covers a total area of 916,445 km2 where about 31,518,855 people live. The people in this country are renowned players in beauty pageants and cosmetics industry, as it is a popular pastime of many Venezuelans. In fact the country already has 22 victories in beauty pageants. One of the most popular tourist attractions in Venezuela is the Angel Falls (image above). It is regarded as the highest uninterrupted waterfalls in the world, at 978 meters high. The waterfall is at its highest from June to December.

Vietnam

Official Name: Socialist Republic of Vietnam

Capital City: Hanoi

Vietnam is a country located in Southeast Asia. Its territory covers a total area of 332,698 km2, where an estimated population of 94,444,200 live. It is also regarded as the 14th most populous country in the world. Ha Long Bay (image above) is one of the most beautiful and most popular tourist destinations in Vietnam. It has aqua-green water and huge rocks which seems to rise from the water. This incredibly beautiful bay also contains more than 2,000 islands with enchanting grottoes, caves, sinkholes and lakes.

Yemen

Official Name: Republic of Yemen

Capital City: Sana'a

Yemen is an Arab country in Western Asia. It occupies a total area of 527,970 km2 and has a population around 27,477,600. Socotra is considered the jewel of biodiversity in the Arabian Sea. In the 1990s, nearly 700 kinds of plant and animals are discovered in this country and are found nowhere else on earth. One of the most striking of Socotra's plants is the dragon's blood tree (image above), it is a strange-looking, umbrella-shaped tree, with red sap which was thought to be the dragon's blood of the ancients. Today, this red sap is used as paint and varnish.

Zambia

Official Name: Republic of Zambia

Capital City: Lusaka

Zambia is a landlocked country bordered by the Democratic Republic of the Congo, Tanzania, Malawi, Mozambique, Zimbabwe, Botswana, Namibia and Angola. It covers a territory of 752,618 km2 and has roughly 16,717,332 inhabitants. Victoria Falls (image above), is a waterfall at the border of Zambia and Zimbabwe. It is neither the highest nor the widest waterfall in the world. However, with its combined width of 1,708 meters and height of 108 meters it is classified as the world's largest sheet of falling water.

Zimbabwe

Official Name: Republic of Zimbabwe

Capital City: Harare

Zimbabwe is a landlocked state bordered by South Africa, Botswana, Zambia and Mozambique. It has around 15,966,810 residents on its 390,757 km2 territory. The Great Ruins of Zimbabwe is one of the ancient archaeological sites in the country. It was believed that the city was constructed in 11th century. Today, the city has turned into a ruin where some walls can be seen with height of above 5 meters. It is considered as a best place to visit in Zimbabwe.